To the Ends of the Earth!

Autobiography of Jennifer Johnson

The wonderful story of God's blessing as she and her husband served as Missionary Helpers to Mongolia

Jennifer Johnson

Copyright © 2003 by Jennifer Johnson

To the Ends of the Earth! Autobiography of Jennifer Johnson
by Jennifer Johnson

Printed in the United States of America

Library of Congress Control Number: 2003091653
ISBN 1-591604-14-1

All rights reserved. No part of this publication may be reproduced or transmitted in any form or by any means without written permission of the publisher.

All scripture quotations, unless otherwise indicated, are from the Holy Bible, King James Version.

Consistent with Mongolian naming structure, only first names are used throughout this book.

Proceeds from this book will go to spreading the gospel in Mongolia.

Jenny can be contacted at: hal-jen-johnson@usa.net

Xulon Press
www.xulonpress.com

To order additional copies, call 1-866-909-BOOK (2665).

Karen —
 God bless you as you serve Him at your end of the earth.
  Jenny

Karen

DEDICATION

That the generation to come might know them, even the children which should be born; who should arise and declare them to their children: That they might set their hope in God, and not forget the works of God, but keep his commandments... Psalm 78:6-7

To my grandchildren who at the time of this writing are not yet conceived. I pray that as they read about this exciting journey of their grandparents that they "not forget the works of God but keep his commandments."

May all who come behind us find us faithful.

TABLE OF CONTENTS

Dedication		v
Introduction	God's Timing is Perfect	ix
Chapter One	Traveling Light	15
Chapter Two	Peace That Passes All Understanding	25
Chapter Three	Getting There	31
Chapter Four	Home Where I Belong!	45
Chapter Five	To the Ends of the Earth!	59
Chapter Six	Culture Shock	83
Chapter Seven	Outside My Comfort Zone	93
Chapter Eight	Hair-Raising Adventures	119
Chapter Nine	Teaching Old Tongues New Tricks	125
Chapter Ten	Christmas is Not for Wimps	145
Chapter Eleven	Ready for Take Off	161
Chapter Twelve	Memories of a Year	171
Chapter Thirteen	Normal is Good	175
Chapter Fourteen	Prospering in Health	203
Chapter Fifteen	Religions of Mongolia	209
Chapter Sixteen	Counting the Days Until Furlough	217
Chapter Seventeen	The Honeymoon is Over	237
Chapter Eighteen	Scenes I Cannot Forget	257
Chapter Nineteen	The Rest of the Story	265

Introduction

GOD'S TIMING IS PERFECT

*He hath made every thing beautiful in his time:
also he hath set the world in their heart...Ecclesiastes 3:11*

**Mid-1960's
Youth Rally
Bakersfield, California**

    The speaker preached about sharing the gospel with the whole world. I loved the topic! I had always loved missions - even before I was saved. Missionary presentations with the pictures and artifacts bored some people, but those were my favorite services. When I stopped pretending to be a Christian and asked Jesus into my heart, I was overwhelmed with God's love! The Bible seemed like His personal love letter to me.
    That evening at the Youth Rally the speaker asked young people who were interested in giving their lives for the sake of the gospel to come and stand at the altar. I walked down and stood with the others and sang:

> I'll go where you want me to go, dear Lord.
> 'Oer mountain or plain or sea.
> I'll say what you want me to say, dear Lord.

I'll be what you want me to be.

And I meant that from the bottom of my heart.

In the days that followed, I decided the best way to get to the foreign mission field was to marry a missionary. So I got a course catalog from a Bible College and started to make plans to enroll after I graduated from high school. I was dating Hal. I never told him my ulterior motive for attending Bible College but nonetheless, he was not too thrilled with my plans. I was a strong-willed young lady and I could have pursued my plans if I had wanted to, but I didn't because you see, I had fallen in love with Hal.

So I attended the local junior college and then went to work for Standard Oil Company and began to plan our wedding. In the meantime, Hal had been drafted into the Army. Although this was during the Vietnam War, as a direct answer to my prayers (or so I felt), Hal was one of just three men in his company shipped to Europe - while thousands were being shipped to Vietnam. What were the chances of that happening? Many of the young men who served in Vietnam came home damaged or in body bags. My fiancée returned from Europe after two years and we were married.

1970 - 1980's
Concord, California

God blessed Hal and me with good careers. I ended up with a job that I was not qualified to do. I had neither the education nor the training but with God's help I served as a law firm administrator with the same law firm for 24 years. God blessed me beyond my wildest imagination. What more could I ask for than a challenging, satisfying job that I loved! Hal was also blessed with a good job at Chevron. Oh yes, the Lord dealt bountifully with us!

After ten years of marriage our home was blessed with children. Christopher was born in 1977 and two years later Craig was born. These are two of the most handsome, wonderful children on the face of God's earth! Trust me on that one! Our family was the typical, busy American family. Our days were packed with work (including lots of overtime), school, music lessons, concerts, sports (soccer, track, football and wrestling), church activities galore, a wide variety of ministries and Boy Scouts (the whole family was involved). What exciting, busy days those were!

I had everything a woman could ask for and I was happy. But what about that "altar" experience thing when I was a teenager? Sometimes I pondered if there was a perfect will of God and a permissive will of God. I never discussed it with anyone. God had blessed me with a great family, beautiful children and very satisfying ministries. I decided maybe God was going to fulfill my desire to be a missionary by calling one of my sons to the foreign field - sometime way off in the future. In the meantime I felt I was called to support missions at home.

So as we raised our children, we tried to teach them that missionaries are special people. We were always the first to volunteer to feed or house visiting missionaries. We gave to missions. I wrote to missionary wives. I organized mission programs for ladies' meetings. I sent gifts to the foreign field. Hal visited a mission work in Mexico. Our family visited a mission work in Canada. We were just a good solid, mission-minded church family.

During this time sometimes I sang specials. I would sing:

> My house is full but my field is empty.
> Who will go and work for me today?
> It seems my children all want to stay around my table.
> But no one wants to work in my field.
> No one wants to work in my field.

I don't have a beautiful singing voice so the only redeeming value in my singing specials was if I could minister from the heart. I had to stop singing that song because it was too convicting. I always thought of my "altar experience".

1990's
Martinez, California

In the early 1990's we moved our church membership from the

Concord church to the Martinez church. That was a hard change for us and we didn't really understand at the time, but we knew we had to make the change. Later we could see that God was positioning us for what He had in store for us.

At the Martinez church I was team teacher of a Teacher Training Class - teaching teachers how to teach. I insisted on teaching the unit on missions. After I completed the first session, Vonnie asked "Jenny, did you make a left-turn somewhere in your life?" Dumbfounded I asked what she meant. She said "You taught that topic with so much conviction. I just wondered if you were supposed to be a missionary." I was amazed since no one knew of my desire to be a missionary. I laughed and told her I had made no left turn…..and went home wondering once again about my "altar experience" so many years before. My boys were nearing adulthood. Maybe one of them would be called to the foreign field. But the thought frightened me. Give up one of my boys!! They could end up in some developing country!!! Yet I knew if God wanted to use one of my sons, I had to be willing because just like Hannah in the Old Testament - I had given them to the Lord.

July 1997

We were having dinner with our pastor and his wife celebrating our two wedding anniversaries which are the same time of year. (An interesting observation - we celebrated together that year - never before and never since.) While eating our salads our pastor asked if Hal would like to be a part of a teaching team to Mongolia the following summer. Later I heard him say that he had not given it any prior thought. He asked Hal on the spur of the moment. Without any forethought or consideration, Hal quickly said "Sure". What an exciting, different adventure! I mean who ever heard of anyone actually going to Outer Mongolia?? I knew it was the place farthest from any other place on earth! Hal figured since he wasn't a preacher, he would go along, take pictures, carry luggage and generally be a helper for the other preachers.

July 1998

Hal and five other men spent a week in Mongolia - teaching at a summer camp. Hal had the awesome privilege of being instrumental in one precious soul accepting Christ.

Hal came home from Mongolia with a heavy burden for the people he met. He was asked to lead another short-term teaching team the following year. We talked about it and agreed to do that, but the heavy burden would not go away. So we decided that that short-term trip would also serve as a survey trip. We would then consider moving to Mongolia after we retired in a few years, but the heavy burden still would not go away.

November 9, 1998

We sat in the church parsonage visiting with Dennis and Charlotte. Dennis was on the team that had gone to Mongolia. He had resigned his pastorate in Louisiana and was making plans to go to Mongolia. Dennis announced that he and Charlotte would go to Mongolia the following summer with our teaching team but that they would remain there permanently. Hal looked at me across the room. Several weeks earlier I had realized this was where we were heading. No argument from me. After all, I had given my life for missions over 30 years earlier! I was ready. After so many years of marriage, that communication occurred between us - without words. So Hal announced that we too would move to Mongolia the following year.

Immediately the heavy burden was rolled off our shoulders! We felt free for the first time in weeks! Although we faced a monumental task and life-changing events, we were jubilant!

My times are in thy hand. Psalm 31:15

My "altar experience" now made sense. I had married myself a missionary! I just didn't know it until 30 years later! That seems awfully slow in man's thinking, but God's timing is perfect. I have thought a lot about why it took so long. I don't know. Maybe it took

God that long to prepare us for this place. Maybe God needed mature (real mature!) Christians here in Mongolia at this time. I know as soon as God called us to Mongolia, we didn't dawdle. It was only a matter of a few months until we were heading out on this exciting journey.

This is the story of our move to Mongolia and the early years here. The story is not about us – but about what God is doing in this place – in spite of us. This book is a compilation of letters, emails and other writings (largely unedited) that I prepared each week. Some items were originally written for public reading. Others were written for family and friends. Still other portions of this book are from my private journal – never really intended for others to read but shared here for whatever value they might add.

My desire is to capture the sights, sounds, smells and feelings of this faraway land - so I will never forget…and to try and make the foreign mission field real to those who can never visit….and especially for my precious grandchildren. This book is for them…with much love from Emay (that is Mongolian for Grandma) and Papa Howie (as Hal has been called by children and some adults for almost 20 years.)

To God be the glory. Great things He has done!

Chapter One

TRAVELING LIGHT

November 13, 1998

Dear Mom & Dad:

    I wanted to get this news off to you before you hear it from someone else. Lord willing, we plan to move to Mongolia next July. Instead of going for a short-term trip like we originally planned, we have decided to go next summer and stay. There are dozens of pieces of this puzzle falling into place - in a truly amazing way. I don't have time to share all of them, but believe me when I say that God is putting this together - and has been for a long time.
    Chris and Craig are supportive and excited about our adventure. (Do I have great kids or what?!?) Craig couldn't keep the grin off his face when we told him. As we visit churches where Boundless Joy has been, we are told by the pastors that Chris tells them about what we are doing - as an introduction to our visit. (Boundless Joy was a Southern Gospel group from our sponsoring church. Christopher served as sound technician for them.) So we have our own "advance man" preparing the way for us! The pastor in one church blew Hal away by telling him (right before Hal started his presentation) that it was obvious that Chris was proud of his parents. That is not something a Johnson man would say out loud,

but oh how the message came through loud and clear to that pastor!

We have a lot to get done in eight months - sell the house, sell the cars, get rid of tons of stuff, store some of it, take a little bit of it, buy the special things we will need in Mongolia (like coats rated to 30 degrees below zero), get Craig settled somewhere for school, get systems set up so we can conduct business from afar, get shots, get physicals, get dental work done, get visas.....the list goes on and on. I am calling this the "Mother of All Lists"!

At the office I have 23 years of stuff to sort through before I leave. By the way, they plan to hire two people to replace me - a manager and a computer person. I've always known I have been doing the work of at least two people!

I cannot start to tell you how excited we are about this next phase of our life. Some people comment that we must be frightened. Nope. No fear. Some think it must be hard to leave everything. Nope. It feels right. I know there will be hard times, but I am now living the peace that passes all understanding. Some think we must be anxious. Not a bit. Nothing has ever felt so right!

Someone at work commented that I had such a glow about me. They likened it to the glow of pregnancy and then they commented that I am "giving birth to a new life" literally. After only hearing a few of the details, my boss said "Jenny, this feels like it was meant to be!" So people can see and sense the power of God.

Through this, I have thought - wouldn't Grandad love to see this? I can picture the smile on his face at the thought of his granddaughter sharing the gospel in a far away land. We are literally going to the "uttermost part". *(Acts 1:8)*

Bye. Love you.

Christmas Letter 1998

Dear Friends and Loved Ones:

Sometimes when I prepare holiday letters, I wonder what I could possibly say that is different or interesting. Well, this year that is not a problem! And next year is not going to be a problem either!! For you see, I am absolutely certain that 1998 will be the single most decisive turning point in our lives.

In July Hal went to Mongolia as part of a teaching team. In addition to visiting Beijing (and walking on the Great Wall of China), he spent a week in Mongolia presenting the gospel - in simple, straightforward style. He found the people open and anxious to learn. He will never be the same - nor will I. After returning from his trip and through a series of truly incredible events that reconfirmed to us at every turn that God was in control of an amazing plan, we feel we must move to Mongolia. We will be missionary helpers. The opportunities for service are tremendous in this country that has been under communist rule for seven decades prior to 1990. Hal has informed Chevron and I have informed McCutchen that we will be retiring in June. The normal reaction to quitting jobs after 30 and 23 years respectively would be difficult at best, but we both felt the most incredible peace (the kind that passes all understanding!) when we gave notice.

We are now in the process of presenting the Mongolian work to churches up and down the state of California. We are sorting through our belongings, deciding what to store, what to ship (very little), what to toss and what to sell. We are going to have the "mother of all garage sales"! We hope to have everything in order and leave by mid-July 1999.

So there you have it in a nutshell. God is working in truly amazing ways to change our lives! After so many years of loving missions, giving money to missions, entertaining missionaries in our home and generally having a heart for missions, we are actually getting to go on the field - to a place where many have never heard the name of Jesus - even once!! What a privilege! We are delivering the same message that the angel delivered so long ago as recorded in *Luke 2:10:*

> *I bring you good tidings of great joy which shall be to all people* (even those at the end of the earth - as Mongolia is called).

For unto you is born this day in the city of David, a Savior which is Christ the Lord!

Some have called us brave. Some have called us crazy. Some have called us strange. We are none of those. We are honored to have the opportunity to do this exciting, wonderful work! We can hardly wait to see the things that our awesome God has in store for us!

We pray that your Christmas is a blessed and happy one. Next year I will write my holiday letter from Ulaanbaatar, Mongolia.

Love, Hal, Jenny, Chris and Craig

Hurry! Faster!

As we prepared to go to Mongolia, it seemed God was opening doors faster than we could walk through them! It felt like He was scooting us along saying "Hurry! Faster! I have things for you to do in Mongolia!"

We put our house on the market in February. The first weekend we got two offers - at the full asking price! Escrow closed and we moved out the end of April. I remember the day we finished emptying the house. I vacuumed it one last time and checked every cupboard to be sure we didn't leave anything. It was late evening and I sat down on the back step like I had done so often during the past 18 years we had lived there. I needed to rest and I needed to say goodbye to the house. It was just wood and plaster and paint but the place was rich in memories and we needed closure so we could move on to the new life God had planned for us.

Our boys were 3-1/2 and 1-1/2 years old when we had moved in. Oh the happy times those walls had seen - from toddler antics to high school achievements! I would never again be inside that house. The "old Jenny" would have been distraught, but I didn't cry over that house. One thing I had already learned is that things are not worth crying over. People are - but not things. I was learning how to travel light which is the way I should have viewed life's stuff all along.

At one time I clutched so many things so tightly in my hand – declaring they were important and they were mine! Children, job, accomplishments, ministries! All mine! (They were not mine at all.

They were loaned to me for a short time, but I held to them strongly.) Even before God called us to Mongolia, He began to gently pry open my fist – one finger at a time so that by the time we left, I had released everything I had held so dear. Finally at last I could offer to God – nothing – nothing but my empty open hand. That's all He wants. He doesn't want our ability. He wants our availability. (Thank you, Dennis, for reminding us of this so often.) Finally I was fully available to God. How thankful I am that He is a patient God.

Chevron offered a voluntary severance package and Hal qualified. That was a major answer to prayer. At one point Chevron told Hal he had to remain on the payroll until the end of 1999 in order to get the package. Hal has a great deal of faith and he said "No way. I have my plane ticket for July. I'm leaving whether I get the package or not but I believe I deserve the package." He had dodged Chevron's downsizing bullets for over 30 years. Surely he deserved something for that! He got the package and finished work the week before we boarded the plane. God is the God of all things - even Chevron!

Normally missionaries spend 18 or more months doing deputation and raising support to go on the foreign field. We just felt we didn't have that much time. Apparently God agreed. Our deputation was less than ten months - and the first three months we thought we were only going on a short-time summer trip! Yet God provided all that we needed.

But my God shall supply all your need according to his riches in glory by Christ Jesus. Philippians 4:19

A Secret Letter to Christopher

From the time I was pregnant with each of my sons, every year I tried to find the time to write a letter to them about what they were doing that year. I never gave them the letters. I just put them away for a future time. This was my letter to Christopher in 1999. The crowning event was Chris and Stephanie's wedding in May – right before we left for Mongolia.

To the Ends of the Earth!

June 19, 1999
Dear Christopher:

 This may be my last writing to you secretly. When I started doing this before you were born, my plan was to continue until you married or left home. Of course, I may just continue it. It feels kind of sneaky to be writing and you don't know it, but maybe that's half the fun! I doubt you would enjoy these writings much now anyway. I think they will be most precious to you as you raise children and/or after I am gone.
 Dad and I are sooooo very proud of you! As you stood at the wedding in your tuxedo, waiting for your beautiful bride – the love of your life – I thought my heart would burst with love. I was reminded of the first time I held you in my arms. At that time too I thought my heart would burst because of all the love I felt for you. You – whom I had carried in my body under my heart – for nine months. You – who had kicked my ribs until they were sore. You – who had sat on my bladder those last few weeks before you were born. You – who got stuck in the birth canal and became distressed forcing a Caesarian Section. OK, so that wasn't your fault but mine.
 But once again I felt my heart swell with pride at all you have become - articulate, self-reliant, confident, trustworthy, fun, creative, faithful in service to God, a man of faith. You recently became indignant because some in the church were opposed to sponsoring a new missionary. They were afraid the church would go bankrupt. You disagreed and freely shared your ideas publicly. You believe that God will provide what is needed - that if we step out in faith we have nothing to fear. You said if we get tightfisted and hold back, we will go bankrupt. Where did you get such ideas? Where did your faith come from? I don't know, but I am thankful that you are a young man of faith. I expect great things from you.
 So now you are the head of your household – setting the tone for your home. Providing spiritual leadership for Stephanie. I know you will be a great husband. I see all the characteristics for that.
 I always wondered if I would be jealous of my daughter-in-laws. Early in high school when I first saw a young girl flirt with you, I felt some jealousy. I wanted her to leave you alone. But I can

honestly say that I have absolutely nothing but love for Stephanie. It seems the most natural relationship in the world. Why shouldn't we be good friends? We love the same man! She is the daughter I never had. God is so good. If my faith ever waivers, I can just look at her and see God's answer to prayer. I have been praying for her since before she was born and what a special answer to prayer she is.

I thought it was so neat at your wedding that Bro. Counts prayed for your children – that they would be healthy. To my knowledge that is the very first public prayer for my grandchildren – and what better place than at your wedding!!

I'll close for now. I could go on and on about how special you are (not perfect, but special), but you might get the big head when you read this. So, I'll just say, I love you more than you can possibly comprehend.

Mom

Early July 1999
Dear Joel & Jenna:

(Joel and Jenna and their family are missionaries to Kenya, Africa. I had corresponded with them through the years.)

What an exciting journey we are on. I know I don't have to tell you. You are way ahead of me on this journey. But I am so thrilled that after all these years of writing to missionary wives – I get to be one! I think I told you that we are part of a mission team. Dennis and Charlotte are the missionaries. Hal and I are missionary helpers. We have never seen a job description for missionary helper so we are making it up as we go. We think going two by two is the Bible way of doing missions. All four of us are terribly excited about this.

Deputation has been interesting, challenging, exciting, funny and a huge blessing but it is almost over and we are glad.

Our oldest son, Christopher got married May 29 – to a wonderful Christian girl. The wedding was beautiful! What a glorious day we had! If I had known that attending your kid's wedding was so much fun, I might have had more kids. (Not really, but it sounds good.) Stephanie is the daughter we never had. What a joy she is to us! They are settled in their little love nest in Sacramento with their mountain of wedding gifts. Craig (our youngest) is settled in Chris' old apartment in Sacramento. Both boys will attend Sacramento State in the Fall. Chris has been there two years. Craig is just transferring in.

We have been homeless since the end of April, but boy does God know how to take care of missionaries! Our friend (whose husband died in January) asked us to live with her until we leave for Mongolia. Of the three months, she is traveling two of the months so we are really house-sitting. And what a house we have to sit! It is huge and beautiful. I jokingly say one wing of the house is in one zip code and the other wing is in another zip code. That is a bit of an exaggeration but not much! We have known them for so long and we feel completely comfortable here. We know Bob would be pleased that Anne is doing this. They have always been supportive of missions and God's work in general. What a blessing for us to have such a nice home. I thought it would bother me to be unsettled and have all my belongings in boxes and bags. But God's grace has been more than sufficient. It really hasn't bothered me. I try to keep my bags and boxes in order and I try to make the space right around me – my home – wherever I am.

So we are moving along. I have less than two weeks of work left. We have a few more things to obtain and finish our packing, say goodbye to everyone, get on the plane and get outta here – on to our exciting journey.

Jenna, are you and Joel getting some rest and taking some time for yourself and your family? You know how important that is. The work of the mission will always be there for you to do. I already know this is going to be a major challenge for Hal and Dennis. There is so much to be done in Mongolia and they are both hard-working, driven men. Charlotte and I will be challenged to keep them from working themselves to death over there. Charlotte and I will have lots of opportunities to minister to the women and children also. Thankfully, we are going at a time in our lives when we do not have small children in the home. So we just have to take care of our husbands.

Well, I better shut this down for now. God gave us this wonderful gift of a whole Saturday with no appointments. You can probably imagine how wonderful it feels! Our deputation appointment tomorrow is close by so there is no traveling. The last two weekends were far away and I was sick besides. So today is a wonderful blessing! The weather is perfect to boot!

God bless you richly as you continue to serve Him.

Love, Jenny

Things I Learned

I learned some important lessons during the months leading up to our departure. Nothing profound – just truths that became very real to me.

A house is not a home. Home is a feeling. I learned to carry a couple of pictures of family with me – to put on my night stand. Wherever I am – that is my home.

We humans collect far too much stuff. Things are not important – people are.

Enjoy this moment right now. It is precious!

Jim Elliot, missionary to the Quichua Indians and who gave his life in South America, summed it up beautifully: "He is no fool who gives what he cannot keep to gain what he cannot lose."

Chapter Two

PEACE THAT PASSES ALL UNDERSTANDING

This writing was prepared after being up 40+ hours – except for napping on the plane.

July 28, 1999

My grace is sufficient for thee. II Corinthians 12:9

And the peace of God, which passeth all understanding, shall keep your hearts and minds through Christ Jesus. Philippians 4:7

I lived these two verses in the most awesome way imaginable. The last week in the States was stressful as we finished our packing – throwing away more stuff than anyone could imagine, leaving behind things I really wanted to take to Mongolia, and trying to cram everything into Action Packers. (Action Packers are large plastic containers. I think they were designed just for missionaries. They not only get you to the field - they serve as various pieces of furniture after you get there!) Then add to that the many, many goodbyes and it was probably one of the most difficult weeks of my life. But through it all, I never felt totally overwhelmed. God said He would be with us through the deep water *(Isaiah 43:2)* and He and I did some heavy tredding that last week.

Then the week culminated in finally leaving. I had always known that saying goodbye to Chris and Stephanie and Craig would be the absolute hardest part of going to Mongolia.

Harder than putting Muffin to sleep. Muffin was our 12 year old, blind Cocker Spaniel. No one would take her. I even tried to sell her at our garage sale. I offered to pay people to take her, but we had no takers. So even though she was in good health except for her blindness, we had to put her to sleep in late April when we sold the house. That was a very difficult thing - to take her to the vet and see her turn her head toward us as we left - not understanding why we were leaving her. If there were a Dog Heaven, Muffin would be there because she gave her life for the sake of missions.

Harder than selling the house.

Harder than getting rid of almost everything we owned.

Harder than saying goodbye to church family.

Harder than calling Mom and Dad one last time.

The hardest. I will never forget saying goodbye to my children and how God worked in such a mighty way. After several hugs and kisses, I waved goodbye, crawled into the van, gave them one last "I love you" sign in sign language and we headed for the airport and everything was OK. My tears stopped before we got out of the church parking lot. There was pain, but there was a peace like I've never felt before!

Oh that peace! I don't understand it. I can't explain it. But I have lived it! Philippians 4:7 is marked in my Bible with the notation "July 1999" – not the date of a sermon I heard or some truth I learned intellectually but the date that I LIVED that verse!

I had refused to allow our children to go to the airport with us. I didn't think I could handle that. So we said goodbye to them at the parsonage along with dozens of other friends. Bill and Rosie and Rosie's mother took us to the airport and Anne and Elaine insisted on going even though it was very late at night. They just simply would not respond to any of my very logical reasoning of why they should stay home. What a special memory that is.

At the airport we walked toward our waiting area and because of security reasons, they could not join us. It was a very long corridor.

We hugged – long and hard - and turned to go to our gate. Every few steps I turned to look back and they were still there waving to us. I kept turning around. They kept waving. They would not leave as long as we were in sight. They got smaller and smaller as I walked away but they never left. They stood and waved until the corridor turned and we were out of sight. God has truly blessed us with wonderful friends!

Eleven hours on the plane – almost all in darkness. Eating at strange intervals, trying to sleep in a narrow airplane seat. But actually it didn't seem like eleven hours. Then four hours in the Seoul Airport.

In Another World

We arrived in Beijing. What an experience! (Beijing now has a beautiful modern airport. This arrival was at the old airport.) The big huge modern airplane stopped out on the tarmac and all the passengers maneuvered their carry-ons while teetering down long wobbly stairs onto the tarmac. The weather was about 90 degrees, 90% humidity and smoggy and oppressive.

While standing on the tarmac with huge airplanes taxiing just a few feet away (complete with all the screaming of the engines and the hot air off the engines – like we would notice), I observed my surroundings. Around the airport were very old single-story brick buildings. They reminded me of army barracks. They were very much in need of repair with broken windows and weeds and generally run down. There were bars on all the windows. I saw a hammer and sickle painted on one of them. Very depressing.

The bus came and we crammed onto it. There were a few seats but most of us stood for the short ride to the terminal. The terminal looked like a huge metal Quonset hut. It had to be the ugliest airport terminal in the world. Inside (still very hot – no air conditioning or fans), the first thing we did was stand in line to have our passports checked. There were probably 20 lines – all with dozens of people standing in them. Some people tried to crowd. Some "ladies of the night" cut in line in front of Dennis and Charlotte and the authorities didn't like that much. There was a ruckus that held up Dennis and Charlotte and made Charlotte a little concerned about what kind of mood the officer would be in, but they finally got through.

In the meantime Hal and I got our passports checked and went to get the luggage – 19 pieces in total! As it came off, Hal pulled it off the conveyor belt and shoved it about ten feet toward me. I started stacking and grouping our luggage near a pole. I had to do this with my bag on my back because my money was in my bag and I had to take a few steps away from the collection of luggage to retrieve each piece Hal shoved to me. Some of the Action Packers weighed 65 pounds. I didn't know I could handle that much weight but I had no choice so I did. All the Action Packers made it fine. One took some serious abuse but after we got to Mongolia we learned that nothing got broken. We were glad we strapped the Action Packers in addition to the locks because that one would surely have popped open.

After getting all the bags, we put them on airport carts – about three or four to a cart. We had a total of five carts. We had to push them through inspection. They only scanned a few of them. We only dumped them a couple times trying to push the carts. Then we were outside the terminal in the oppressive heat which included car exhaust and smokers lighting up after their long flights. The drivers and pedestrians were all nuts.

Hal found the representative from the hotel where we were going to stay. The first van came and we put about half the bags on the van. Dennis, Charlotte and I went on that van. Hal came on the next van with the rest of the stuff. I wasn't thrilled about Hal being separated from the rest of us but we didn't have a choice.

The van was so crowded with our stuff and a few other passengers that I sat with one cheek on a seat and the other cheek on Dennis' computer case in the aisle. Dennis had to stand in the doorway of the bus. The Action Packers were stacked so high that when the driver applied the brakes, the one in the front seat slid forward and would have hit the driver in the head if Dennis and I had not held it. In the back, one Action Packer would slide when the van turned left and would have hit Charlotte in the head except a very nice passenger held it in place.

We were all sweating like pigs. Perspiration was running down the small of my back and between my ... well, you get the picture! My shirt was stuck to my shoulder blades because of sweat. The driver did not speak English but would occasionally look at Dennis (balancing in the doorway with sweat dripping off his chin) and shake his head and laugh – not in mockery – just in disbelief! Dennis smiled back meekly.

The drive to the hotel was short but oh my goodness – what a strange place. Poverty everywhere. Houses that were shacks and stores that were huts. Lots of little pickups – reminding me of an old war movie. I got to see the crazy drivers from the front seat of the van.

We pulled onto the grounds of the hotel and it was like entering a foreign world – a refreshing, wonderful world. A world class hotel in the middle of a ghetto. I was so thankful to be there safe and sound – with all of my stuff.

God is so good to us! I can't even start to express how much He has done for us and how confident we are that this is what God wants us to do right now. What an exciting journey we are on!

> What a mighty God we serve.
> What a mighty God we serve.
> Angels bow before Him.
> Heaven and earth adore Him.
> What a mighty God we serve.

Chapter Three

GETTING THERE

July 30, 1999
Beijing, China

I don't think I actually missed a day journaling. I think I was confused when I wrote July 28. I think it was really July 29 but who knows? We had this huge chunk of unbroken time somewhere late in July.

We have been told that the best way to get your body clock reset after jet lag is to try very hard to sleep on the correct time of where you are. So we all sat in the lobby after dinner that first night – totally numb from lack of sleep and our body clocks soooo messed up. But we knew if we went to our rooms, the sight of beds would be overwhelmingly tempting. So we sat in the lobby like zombies. It seems that my ears and eyes were not functioning – probably out of respect for my poor brain that was shut down. No more input could be processed through that gray mass. Finally we wandered off to bed around 8:00 p.m.

I awoke after a while and after using the bathroom decided I wanted to know what time it was. I looked for my watch in the dark but could not find it. I found Hal's. It said 2:30. I moaned and went back to bed and tried very hard to go back to sleep. I needed to sleep through the night. I felt so rested. I could not force myself to sleep. When I thought about where I was and the exciting journey I was on, I just grinned in the dark. A while later, Hal woke up and asked what time it was. I told him it was probably around 3:00 a.m. He moaned and said "see, I told you we went to bed too early". I reluctantly admitted he was right. Then he turned the light on and looked at the alarm clock which read 6:00 a.m. We had in fact slept through the night! Hal's watch was still on California time!!

We began our day with devotions and prayers in Dennis and Charlotte's room. What a joy to have our team together at last. Dennis read the passage about leaving father, mother and children to serve God. Boy, does that scripture now have new meaning! But we are all rejoicing that we have the opportunity to do this.

We had a wonderful breakfast (included with the room) and then we took the shuttle downtown. We are in this beautiful oasis of cleanliness and European style hospitality. As soon as we drive outside the compound or village, it becomes immediately clear that we are in a very poor country.

People everywhere – millions of them. Housing is either very luxurious or tiny brick hutches that look barely fit for animal shelter. There is simply no middle class at all. Almost everything is very dirty. Filthy actually.

Traffic was an experience. Thousands of cars, buses, bicycles and three-wheeled cycles with carts all pushed and shoved and "elbowed" through intersections. Clearance between cars was usually a mere inch or two. I am not exaggerating! Horns honking. If the lanes in the road were marked, no one observed them. It was literally a "root, hog or die" situation.

One time our driver came to an intersection that had a light. It was red. It happened that there was no cross traffic. He did not turn his head either direction nor slow down. In fact he gunned it and we went through on the red! It took everyone's breath away. I praise God for protection. I think God has dispatched a few extra guardian angels for us this week. By the way, we never saw a single accident! And the cars do not have dents, scrapes or dings – not even the taxis! How do they do it?

We shopped at a department store and found a nice grocery store. They literally sell anything you could possibly want. That is a comfort. So if we get too desperate for things in Ulaanbaatar, a

Getting There

quick trip to Beijing will certainly fill the bill.

Charlotte and I are not avid shoppers (thankfully), but we thought we could use another cotton knit shirt for our trip. We went to the ladies section and found one we liked. The sales clerk bluntly said "We do not carry large sizes." Fortunately, Charlotte and I are not overly sensitive. But we would not be denied. We promptly walked to the men's department and picked up the same cotton knit shirt and bought a large – which was just right for us. Tenacity and creativity are nice characteristics in these situations.

We walked to the silk market. There were beggars along the street. The one that bothered all of us was the woman who urged us to take her young son. That broke our hearts. We are not judgmental toward the Chinese. In America, unwanted children are sucked into a sink (in the words of Dr. Laura).

Again yesterday it was extremely hot and humid. We would walk a few blocks and get something to drink. Walk a few blocks and get something to drink. My passport pouch (which was around my neck) was soaked all of the time. Hal has never liked McDonald's but I tell you it was a welcome respite yesterday. They had air conditioning! Then we walked a few more blocks and found a Baskin Robbins – with air conditioning! We may become great fans of American franchises!

Last night we had Peking Duck – well they call it Beijing Duck now. It was pretty good. I'm glad I had it – once. They roast the duck after blowing air between the skin and the meat. The skin is very crispy. Then they carve it at your table. They put chunks of duck, a special black sauce, zucchini and onion in a tortilla. Well they call them pancakes, but they were like flour tortillas. You then dip the "duck burrito" in a sauce. We had vegetables also – black mushrooms and kale and broccoli and snow beans. All of this with chopsticks. Hal has always been good with chopsticks and I guess my ten-day visit in Taipei paid off. I managed to eat with only a little irritation!

They served us tea that looked like things you would dig out of a garbage disposal. Anyway the young man (dressed in bright yellow pajama type outfit) brought a copper water pot with a pour spout that was probably three feet long. The water spurted out of the spout about three or four inches beyond the end of the spout. He stood back from our table and aimed the spout and only once missed the cup. A real talent! A real show!

Dennis asked the waitress to teach us how to order and how to eat. She sweetly but firmly told Dennis "I am waiter. Not teacher." What wonderful laughter God is giving us. So refreshing.

We continue to have a marvelous time. Hard to believe I am actually living this adventure!

The masses of people reminded me of the passage – at the name of Jesus, every knee shall bow and every tongue confess that Jesus Christ is Lord. We want to teach them to bow their knee now – rather than wait to be forced in the hereafter.

We are rested and ready for another wonderful day!

August 1, 1999
Beijing, China

So much happening that I missed a day. I'll try to catch up. Friday we took a walk in the morning – to the village just outside the hotel compound. It is like two different worlds. The hotel is a beautiful European-style luxurious hotel with everything you could want or need. It is kept immaculate by people who clean all day long. Just a few steps away is a poor village of Chinese who live in filth and dirt. There are shops and street vendors. The streets are dirt with potholes. No curbs or sidewalks. We walked a few blocks and came to a park which was nice. Watched a man fly a kite. We felt no wind but he managed to get the kite way up in the air. A group of Chinese were playing a card game. The main activity of everyone was to try and stay cool – which is not easy with the heat and humidity. We were out about one hour and came back drenched completely, red in the face, sweat dripping – and all we did was walk slowly!

After cooling down a bit we took the shuttle downtown to the Friendship Store. From there we hailed a cab and handed him the note in Chinese that said "take us to train station". Egi was arriving by train from Ulaanbaatar and we were to meet him there. When Hal and Dennis visited Mongolia in 1998, they met Egi's wife,

Getting There

Naara and their children. Egi was living in San Francisco at the time. After Bill, Hal and Kevin visited him, he attended our sponsoring church in Martinez until he returned to Mongolia in April 1999. He became our Mongolian helper.

The cabs are teeny-tiny – designed for two in the back and maybe a small person in the front. (The driver is inside a Plexiglass cage.) Well we put Dennis - our "small" one in the front – because we certainly did not need him in the back. Hal, Charlotte and I squeezed in the back (designed for two). But we did not want to be split up. It took about 20 minutes to get to the train station but it wasn't that far. Most of the time we were in gridlock traffic.

The train station was our first time out with no one who speaks English. The station is huge, very old, and in need of repair with thousands of people milling about and all the signs in Chinese. After four attempts to communicate and wandering around the station several times, we got enough information to figure out where to meet arriving passengers. We never did see a train although Dennis said he got a glimpse of one while he was inside. We worried that we might miss Egi. We decided we should make a sign that we could hold above our heads. As we walked along, I found a piece of cardboard and picked it up. We used an old lipstick of mine augmented by Charlotte's lipstick pencil to write "Egi" in large letters. We were just beginning to learn the extent of our ingenuity!

People stared at us openly. No wonder. We were there for over an hour and I only saw two Caucasian men and one Caucasian woman. At first we wondered if the guys' flies were open but then realized they just found our faces interesting. It could be they were fascinated with our sweating. I swear we sweat three times more than the natives. Egi doesn't sweat at all! We tease him that he doesn't even get wet under the shower! He just grins good naturedly!

We found Egi. So good to see him again. Gave him a big hug. Then we walked all the way back to the Friendship Store chattering with Egi all the way. It was just over one kilometer. We learned that our next challenge was to get Egi a return ticket. Apparently, you can only buy one-way train tickets. No such thing as roundtrip and you can only buy tickets three days before departure. (We soon learned that lack of planning or forethought is a given in Asia. An amazement to us!) Egi tried to get a ticket from a friend at a hotel. No go. We then walked to Baskin Robbins for ice cream. Praise the Lord some of America has arrived in China!

Yesterday, we hired a driver to take us sightseeing. It is more cost effective than taking individual tours. However, we did not get a guide and our driver speaks only Chinese. He took us to Tiannamen Square, Forbidden City, cloissone factory (including lunch – the best Chinese food I have ever eaten) and then to the Great Wall. We all walked on it. The men went farther than Charlotte and me. We are smart enough to know when to stop. Egi and Dennis went way up to a far tower. Hal went part way and came back down (thankfully). I didn't want to deal with heat stroke. Guzzling water helps. What an incredible structure the wall is! And to think it was built so long ago to keep the Mongolians out of China! So glad I have had the opportunity to see all this! Just some of the fringe benefits of being a missionary. (There are many!)

During mission training, Brenda talked to us about having a DRA (dirty rotten attitude). Well when we walked on the Great Wall, there was a camel standing just outside the wall. He was chewing his cud in a bored fashion but when I got even with him, we made eye contact (I think) and he stopped chewing and stared at me in a disgruntled sort of way. (That is the only way a camel can look.) He just glared as if to say "Mess with me and I'll spit on you!"

After Charlotte and I ran out of steam and stopped to rest while the men climbed farther up the wall, we got to talking and decided that for the Mongolian Team instead of having a DRA, we will have a CA (Camel Attitude) – glaring, bad mood, threatening to spit. Of course, as you can imagine, Charlotte and I dissolved into giggles. We laughed until we cried which blended with the sweat pouring off our faces.

Our God is so good – meeting all of our needs, including mine and Charlotte's need to laugh!

Today (Sunday) was a day for worship and rest. Good services this morning. At breakfast I saw a man reading his Bible so I approached him. He was a college student from Cincinnati. He and eight friends were returning from a summer ministry in the Chinese countryside. He sprained his ankle and could not join them on sightseeing. He joined us for church instead. It was so nice to have visitors in our first worship service abroad and we had a good time too. Singing praises to God, praying and preaching – all in the hotel room with one visitor and Egi and us four!

It rained this afternoon. Hope it cools things off a bit. I doubt it will. The humidity will probably be worse than ever!

**August 2, 1999
Beijing, China**

After a wonderful, restful day on Sunday, we got up Monday – ready for the challenge of the day - getting our luggage delivered to the freight company to deposit on the train tomorrow! The hotel provided a large van (bigger than the one from the airport). The bell boys helped us stack our bags in and then we all climbed in.

The driver drove like all other Chinese – crazy and aggressive. He stopped twice to ask directions. We were near the train station but he couldn't find the freight company. Finally we went down a back street – very narrow. Then we turned into a back lane even narrower. The van barely fit – with an inch or so clearance on each side. Brick buildings lined the street. At the end of the lane was a brick structure a little bigger than the others. We unloaded our Action Packers and bags. About six or eight men stood around jabbering over our bags. We wondered if they were discussing how much money our stuff would bring at the local flea market!

We had prayed intently over this aspect of our trip and once again God answered our prayers. One of the men spoke Mongolian and Chinese and Egi speaks Mongolian and English. We had to put Dennis and Charlotte's bags in white wrapping stuff and sew them shut. Then we had to affix two tags to each piece. Then each piece was weighed. Then they weighed Dennis and laughed at his 129 k. OK, so we are providing entertainment for the locals.

While this was going on a Chinese lady practiced her English on us. She said she learned English from listening to the radio. She was good. Charlotte and I can't imagine learning all that from radio!

Paying was interesting. We didn't have enough Yuan even

pooling all our money! We gave the man American dollars to take to be exchanged. He took our money and immediately ran down the street. We wondered if we had made a big mistake in judgment. Amazingly he returned in just a few minutes with Yuan. If he had decided to take off with our money, there was absolutely nothing we could have done and no proof that we gave him the money because he took it and left so quickly. God was watching over us – once again!

Then we had to leave our passports and train tickets with them until 3:00 p.m. We did that, again wondering if it was wise. At 3:00 Dennis and Egi went back and got our papers. Dennis witnessed to the Chinese lady who spoke English. She said she had an English Bible.

We went to bed early after having a hamburger on the bun (as it was described on the menu). Not bad. Not American but not bad.

Our time in Beijing had been wonderful. We saw the masses of people who need Christ and we pray that someday China will be open to the gospel and we pray that someone goes there to witness to them. But we have our calling. We know where we belong and it was time to get there.

August 3, 1999
Train from Beijing to Ulaanbaatar

We got up at 4:30 and were ready to leave the hotel by 5:30. The driver was worse than usual. Maybe he was mad about being up so early. We arrived at the train station at 6:30. After a couple of attempts, we found the place where the Ulaanbaatar train leaves. There were masses of people!

Our long trip into Mongolia was on an ancient Chinese-made train. In our tiny compartment, there were two benches about six feet long facing each other with places to stow carry-ons underneath. On the end near the window was a table – for eating or whatever. Then above the benches were two bunk style cots that pulled down. We splurged and got a "soft seat" compartment instead of a "hard seat" compartment. Soft seats had maybe 1/4 inch of padding which disappeared after the first hour of bumping along. However,

Getting There

we were thankful for what little padding we had. We couldn't imagine how "hard seats" felt.

The window opened. That was a blessing since it was hot! They brought us clean sheets and pillow cases. That was a blessing since the pillows were filthy! We were glad it was not cold. The blankets were nasty!

There was hot water at the end of each car but we didn't have cups. If we had read our travel book, we would have known to bring a cup. Dennis got so desperate for coffee, he cut a large water bottle in two and used the bottom half for a "cup", using his handkerchief as a potholder. It melted and bent out of shape a bit, but we were all happy that Dennis got his coffee.

The first hour of the trip, we were in Beijing - a huge town that stretches for miles - with masses of people everywhere. Then we went through the Bodaling Pass where we could see the Great Wall – which we had walked on few days before. With no warning we entered absolutely pitch black tunnels and just as quickly exited into bright sunlight. The mountains were lush and green. Sometimes we had rock walls and trees within inches of the train.

At one point we stopped and changed directions (or so it seemed). I think we actually changed from going west to going north. The engine car moved from one end of the train to the other – on a side track.

The mountains gave way to fields – rice, corn and unknown crops - green and lush. There were little villages in between. Rural China was far more beautiful than I expected. Charlotte and I fell asleep. Dennis and Hal wandered down to the dining car and left us sleeping with our stuff.

When we awoke, the scenery was more desert like. It reminded me of Arizona or New Mexico. There were green fields but in the distance, the hills were brown and arid. It must have been the edge of the Gobi Desert. Some areas reminded me of Central California with crops in the midst of brown hills. We crossed a wide, dried-up river. The desert terrain then changed into a wide, endless plain - green and beautiful. We were so thankful for cool weather. If it had been warmer, the tiny compartment would have been sweltering.

Dennis and Hal flirted with a little Mongolian girl in our car.

To the Ends of the Earth!

She was adorable but she wouldn't talk to them except with her eyes and of course she took the food they offered.

After a lunch of crackers, cookies and water, we decided to "eat out" for dinner. We went to the dining car and had Sweet and Sour Pork with rice. It was pretty good so long as I didn't think about anything. Service was slow but who cares? We were on that train for 30+ hours anyway.

Delicious Peaches!

At train stations in rural China, when the train pulls in, the local natives rush to the train window, pushing a cart to sell their wares. At one stop we bought bottled water that was icy. Oh, that was good since it was quite hot on the train.

At one station Dennis hung out the window and bought a bag of peaches. They were small and hard and not very colorful, but they caught Dennis' eye. That second morning on the train when we were totally sick of crackers and cookies and nuts, we decided to have the peaches for breakfast. We knew they needed to be washed before being peeled so that contaminants from the skin would not be carried into the fruit by the knife. We were resourceful. One of us held a small hand towel under the peach while one of us sparingly poured bottled water over the peaches and one of us rubbed the peaches with the water. We then peeled the peaches with my Swiss Army knife and sliced them. They were absolutely delicious! So obviously you can't tell a peach by its skin.

So if anyone ever asks you how many Baptists it takes to clean a peach, you know the answer: Three (with one person to supervise)!

After seeing some of the other compartments, I was thankful for our own private compartment. Some people smoke in the cars. Ugh! Some of the people have strong body odor (which we four will have by the time we get off, but at least I know we started out clean).

The sunset was absolutely gorgeous! What beautiful countryside! I noticed the number of villages was decreasing. We must be approaching the ends of the earth.

Appreciation for Chinese Ingenuity

Our compartment had bunk beds that catapulted out from the wall above the benches. They were held to the wall with a tiny L bracket. It looked like maybe a ten year old could sleep up there but Dennis decided the guys should sleep on the bunks! Watching him get on the top bunk was exciting. Charlotte wisely joined us on our side of the compartment while Dennis climbed up on his bunk. After it held for a few minutes, she felt it was safe to return to her bed underneath. Amazingly, it held his weight. He had to be careful where he put his hand because there was a circulating fan mounted to the ceiling near the head of his bed.

After watching that bunk hold Dennis, I had a new respect for Chinese ingenuity!

Changing Wheels

At the border, the train pulled into a building. Each car was jacked up and the wheels were changed. The gauge of track is different in China than in Mongolia. The process takes one to two hours.

Even though it was midnight Hal and Egi got off the train and went shopping for fresh fruit at a nearby village. Dennis, Charlotte and I stayed on the train. It bumped, jolted, jarred, jerked and banged as they worked on the train. Dennis hung his head and upper body out the window and watched as they used hydraulic jacks to raise the car. The wheels were held on by a single pin. They rolled one set of wheels off and another set on.

We heard the difference in gauge of track was to stop troop movement. Troops have not moved across these plains in decades (if ever) yet every train goes through this process to this very day!

Mind Over Matter

There was a toilet at the end of the car that was indescribably stinky! I don't know why it smelled so bad since everything was disposed of. After you went (quickly unless you could hold your breath a long time), when you flushed, the bottom of the toilet opened up and the contents dumped out on the track. You could see the train tracks whizzing by!

Charlotte and I avoided going to the toilet. At 9:30 p.m. we had only gone once in 15 hours! Then the train stopped to have the wheels changed and we couldn't go because the door was locked. (That made sense. We would have been going in the building where the wheels were changed so they locked the toilet door.) When the train again started, we visited the disgusting place. We never dreamed we could hold it so long! We learned that when you are desperate enough, you can tolerate even a horrid odor!

Guardian Angel

After the wheels were changed, we stretched out on our "soft beds" to sleep – or so we thought. Soon a uniformed official banged on our door and in a very officious manner checked our passports. We settled down to sleep again.

Soon there was another bang on our compartment door and another very important acting officer wanted to check our declaration papers. She insisted in no uncertain terms that Dennis crawl down from the bunk for this process. We saw no reason for that but of course Dennis complied. All was OK and we settled back down to sleep.

A third time, the officials made us get up – to inspect our compartment to be sure no one was hiding under our benches.

Now you like to think – this is 1999. I am an American. I have a valid passport and properly issued visa. I have not broken the law. There is nothing to be frightened of. But the behavior of the officials brought back snatches of WWII movies. And although we had committed our lives into God's hands, we generally felt uneasy each time they banged on our door in the middle of the night.

A few minutes later there was another knock on the door, but this time the person gently opened it themselves instead of making us get up to do it. I was looking upside down ... at Egi! His hair was tousled, his clothes wrinkled and it was obvious, he had been sleeping, but in his soft voice he wanted to be sure we were OK. He said

Getting There

he had talked to the officials to be sure our belongings (all our Action Packers – located somewhere else on the train) were OK. The fact that the train officials knew about our freight meant that our stuff had made it on the train! This was our first indication that the gabbering guys had not taken all our earthly belongings to the local Chinese flea market! God was watching over us and our stuff.

I always wondered what a guardian angel looked like. At this point in time, he looked like Egi!

Finally after several hours, we completed the stop/start, forward/back, check the passport nuisance. At last we slept - to the gentle swaying rhythm of an ancient train slowly making its way to the land of our calling.

First Glimpse of Our New Homeland

We awoke to the sun coming through the train window. Our less-than-youthful bodies were stiff but refreshed. We got cleaned up as best we could and straightened the cabin. Dennis brought a devotional and we had prayer. It was cool and breezy, cloudy and overcast. Praise the Lord! We were already dirty enough without adding more sweat to the mix!

From the train window I saw my first Mongolian horse, camel and ger – the white round tents most Mongolians call home. The tents are warm in the winter and easily breakdown for moving – which the Mongolians do several times a year. In all my life I never once dreamed that I would get to travel to such a faraway place or see such exotic sights! What an exciting journey I am on!

Chapter Four

HOME WHERE I BELONG!

August 4, 1999
Ulaanbaatar, Mongolia

We arrived in Ulaanbaatar early afternoon. Exhausted, dirty, smelly and numb from the "soft seats" on the train. Naara and Tsambaa together with Dogi met us with flowers for Charlotte and me. What a wonderful way to be greeted! Dogi is a young lady Hal met in 1998. She and I began to correspond by email even before we committed to come to Mongolia. So Dogi is my oldest Mongolian friend. We didn't recognize her because she looked so different from her pictures! I excused myself and stepped around her - only to have her chase me down and call me by name. I have one friend in Mongolia and I don't recognize her! How embarrassing!

God can make seeing eyes blind!

God watched over every step of our move to Mongolia. When the customs officer saw our pile of Action Packers, she asked Dennis and Hal to open the one that she selected so she could inspect it and determine how much duty we owed. We had listed that our bags contained clothing and personal belongings. We had brought computers, printers, cameras – all manner of things that customs officers might want to charge duty on. So when they opened the Action Packer she specified, they held their breath. On top was some of my obviously used clothes. She ran her hand down all four sides and found nothing but clothes. She was satisfied and waived all the luggage through without duty!

When Dennis and Hal came walking up to us, grinning and told us what had just happened, I checked the inventory list and there were several pieces of computer equipment in the Action Packer she checked. A week later when I opened that one, I don't see how the customs officer found only clothing. Was she blind? I think God just wanted to give us one more little reminder that He was with us.

Praise God for Small Favors

We took a taxi to a hotel - thankful for a place to call home until we found an apartment. We rested and cleaned up. After 30+ hours on the train, a shower never felt so good! Just to be clean again was a blessing! I discovered that the foreign field makes you appreciate the simple things in life - like a shower. I can't begin to count the number of times since 1999 that I have stood under a shower and thanked God for hot water – something I never did once when I lived in America!

We ate dinner in the hotel restaurant downstairs. We were their only customers, but the food was excellent and fresh! OK, so we were probably overly hungry. We ventured out for our first look at the place we were going to call home. We went all the way to the State Store which was not far. (See Chapter 9 for a list of definitions of Mongolian phrases like "not far".) The store was closed. We found a pizza place and saw our first Buddhist lama in his robes. The people seemed friendly toward us.

The street noise died down before midnight and Hal and I slept like rocks. Do rocks sleep? Anyway, it started raining in the wee hours of the morning. Is there anything better than sleeping to the sound of rain outside? I don't think so. What a wonderful welcome to our new homeland!

Home Where I Belong!

How strange! Not like me at all!

We never moved around much during our marriage – maybe changing houses but seldom changing neighborhoods. In 1971 when Chevron moved us from Southern California to the Bay Area, it took me over a year to feel at home. I liked our new home and I really wanted to be there. However, I would look around my house and see all my stuff but it didn't feel like home.

Here I was in a place where everything was strange – sights, sounds, smells, language, food, products, housing, music, people – everything. With not one familiar thing in sight, I immediately felt at home. Only God can do that! I endured a lot of adjustments and culture shock but through it all, God gave me an assurance that I was home where I belonged. Praise Him for that!

August 5, 1999
A Fascinating New Life

Our hotel room looked out on a ger village. From my window I watched the city wake up. A man went to the outdoor toilet. Another man urinated in the grass facing the street (and me). A family bathed outside. A young woman came to the door of the ger in her bra and bikini panties. She looked all around for several minutes and checked the weather. All these people were totally unaware and uncaring that I was watching. A fascinating way of life.

We had a very good breakfast downstairs. Cucumber, tomato and sliced meat, juice (or so I thought), bread with butter and jam, flat omelet thing and coffee.

Is there anything more beautiful?

I've seen the American flag at church, on buildings – all over the place – and never thought anything about it. Many times I looked at it without seeing it. Sometimes at ballgames I would get teary-eyed during the National Anthem, but I've never seen anything more beautiful than when we rounded the corner and Dennis said "There's Old Glory!" That was the most beautiful flag I have ever seen! We are safe and fine but I'm so glad our Embassy is there!

We went to the bank only to learn we had to go to another branch to do business. We walked through the center of town with government offices and the main square. We finally found the bank branch and got our accounts open in about an hour – with Egi's help. Can you imagine how long it would have taken without a translator?!

The Oldest Telephones I Have Ever Seen

In the flurry of leaving Martinez, the new digital camera that the McCutchen partners got me as a farewell gift got shoved under a car seat. I remembered it halfway through our long flight to Asia. I called the children from Beijing. UPS assured them they could get it to us within a week. Yeah, right! I was gullible back in those days and believed them. Now I know that nothing can be delivered in Asia that promptly. So while we were traveling to Mongolia, my camera was headed for China. I needed to make a phone call to see if it had arrived at the hotel in China.

We did this from the phone station at the post office because our hotel did not have long distance service. You estimate the length of your call and pay based on that estimate. Then you take the paid receipt to an operator who sits at a switchboard like the one I operated at the high school back in the mid-1960's. There were cords and little holes that you put the telephone cord into and then opened the key to talk or push the key to ring the phone. That is the style of the first switchboards ever made.

Then you wait your turn. It can be up to two hours but we only waited 20 minutes. The operator places the call, rings a numbered phone booth and announces your name and booth number. You run to the correct booth and pick up the ringing phone and conduct your call. My call failed to go through twice so I had to repeat the procedure and each time my phone booth was on the mezzanine. (It was good exercise.) The telephone instrument looked like the first phone ever made in Russia with no buttons or dials. Just a black instrument with a handset you pick up. When your paid time is up, your call is cut off.

Afternote: After much haggling, Christopher got the camera shipped back to the States where he retrieved it. I got it in March 2000 when the church sent us some stuff in Action Packers.

The search for an apartment begins.

A man met us at the hotel to show us an apartment for rent. It was located on the sixth floor of a tall building. The elevator smelled like urine and the hallway was dark. (I later learned that most elevators in Mongolia smell like urine and all hallways are dark.) The first door was metal with several locks and the second door was wooden with several more locks. (I also learned later that all apartments in Mongolia have at least two doors and multiple locks.)

In any other city, this would be considered a ghetto. But in order to have a ghetto, you must have something better in comparison. In Ulaanbaatar everything is about the same so there are no areas considered ghettos. This building was very run down, in need of repair and poorly lit, but Dennis and Hal said it was better than what they had seen in 1998. Charlotte and I wondered if we could ever get the place clean. The smell of smoke and mutton seemed to permeate everything.

Charlotte and I were not overly impressed with the apartment even though Egi said it was very nice. We told him we wanted to see some others. He thought maybe after we saw other apartments, we would realize how good it was. It was at this point that it hit me what a huge challenge it was going to be for us to make a home in this place.

The man who showed us the apartment told us about a language school which would also get us a one-year student visa. We came to Mongolia on 30-day visitor visas so we had to do something – quickly! We never rented that man's apartment but I believe God put him in our lives just to provide us the information about the school.

Precious Memories

We went to dinner at Egi's that evening which will always

remain one of my happiest memories – no matter how long we stay in Mongolia!

Shaka (a friend of Egi's) picked us up in his van. After driving around in circles (or so it seemed) we finally arrived. It was up a dark dank staircase. When the door opened, it was like a ray of sunshine! Their apartment was small (one bedroom for the five of them) but it was clean and comfortable. They had Mongolian Christian music playing. What a joy to recognize melodies even though the words were different. The song "Majesty" was touching as always. The children were adorable. Egi and Naara fixed a fantastic meal with several salads, Japanese BBQ beef, rice, potatoes, bread, cookies and watermelon.

The guys reviewed the translation work Egi had done since returning to Mongolia while Naara, Charlotte and I looked at photo albums. One thing I share with Mongolians – the love of photo albums!

After nightfall we drove to a high hill to see the city lights. There was lots of laughter. At one point, Shaka noticed that there was Dennis and Charlotte, Hal and me and Egi and Naara and then him – the only single person. He put his arms around a light pole and acted like he was going to kiss it! Language is not needed for such humor!

What a wonderful evening with Egi and his family and a mix of Mongolian and English! Charlotte and I had no problem communicating with Naara. She is a delightful lady who loves the Lord and loves her family. Women don't need words. We can communicate with the heart!

August 6, 1999
The search for an apartment continues.

We had breakfast in the hotel again and then walked to the State Store. We were amazed and thankful for what was available. The scrimpy household items we brought with us could be easily supplemented.

Egi met us and we started looking at apartments again. We looked at some in a nicer neighborhood than the area we looked at first. From this area we could see the hills and were reminded of the scripture *I will lift up mine eyes unto the hills, from whence cometh my help. Psalm 121:1*

But the apartments we saw did not intrigue us at all. Egi was trying to be patient with the foreigners he was babysitting. Dennis and Hal were getting irritated with us and didn't try to hide that fact. They told us in no uncertain terms that we were going to have to settle for what we saw. Charlotte and I were getting frustrated because nothing felt right. Men just don't understand women's intuition and things "feeling right".

Then Egi made one more call and we walked into an apartment that was the best we had seen. Not clean but cleaner than the others. Decent carpet. Reasonably new paint. Nice decks. I immediately wanted it. It didn't look that much different from the other apartments we had seen but it felt right. As it turned out, this was the right apartment. God was leading us. See Chapter 11 for details.

Then Egi found a second apartment in the same building for Dennis and Charlotte. We made arrangements to get both apartments on Monday. There was lots of work to be done! The very productive day was capped off with our first Mongolian summer rain storm – one of my very favorite things!

God is our umbrella.

We are so thankful for God's tender care. When we arrived, our conversations with other foreign Christians would go something like this:

> Other Christian: What organization are you with?
> Us: None
> Other Christian (surprised): Really?! What umbrella brought you here?
> Us: God
> Other Christian (with mouth hanging open): Really?! What are you going to do if you get in trouble?
> Us (meekly): Pray

So we quickly learned that most missionaries come to Mongolia under an umbrella organization which makes all their arrangements for living here. We had no such organization. God called us. Our church sent us. We came. We knew nothing about any umbrella except the one we tucked into our suitcase. But we did not suffer. No, not for a minute!

We talked to a family with six children who arrived about the same time we did. She asked if we had our belongings yet. We said "Well, yes. We brought everything with us." She said "Oh that's right, you are the ones who don't have an umbrella organization." (Yea, that would be us!) She then went on to tell us how their container was hung up in customs. The government demanded a ridiculous amount of duty which their umbrella organization couldn't afford to pay. All they had were light jackets until late October because their winter coats and boots were in the container.

Months after we arrived I was talking with another missionary family who arrived the same week that we did. He marveled at all that we had done so quickly. They lived in a hotel several weeks and had moved twice before finding a suitable apartment. It took them months to get long distance phone service and even longer to get a post office box because the post office told them they had none available. When I heard this, I asked Egi about the day we got our post office box. He said he just walked up and asked the clerk and she said normally they didn't have any boxes available but "it just so happened" that a box had just become empty!

I don't believe in coincidence. God was directing our steps through those early days. The God who called us, cared for us – and continues to care for us to this very day! I like our umbrella just fine!

Saturday, August 7, 1999

We spent the day walking around town. Hal and Dennis said the city was generally cleaner than it was in 1998 and there was more construction than last year! Charlotte and I were thankful.

We bought food for a Sunday picnic. We ate dinner in the hotel but I didn't eat much. I had struggled with intestinal problems since the day we arrived. Dennis and Charlotte were suffering a bit. Hal – nothing. Grrrr! People with stomachs of steel can be so annoying at times! It turned out that the "juice" they served us for breakfast every morning at the hotel was a fruit powder mixed with tap water. To this day I cannot drink unboiled tap water.

August 8, 1999
Rain never slows down a Mongolian picnic!

We woke up to find we had no water. Oh joy! We used bottled water to wash our faces and brush our teeth. I used the wet wipes given to me by a ladies group in Arkansas – to "bathe". When I received the wet wipes in a gift basket, I never dreamed I would be using them for my entire bath on my first Sunday in Mongolia! Thank you Lord for them – the ladies and the wet wipes.

The hotel restaurant was closed so breakfast was granola bars and water. Then we walked to church where we joined the congregation for a day in the countryside. It poured down rain but the thought never entered their minds to cancel the event. We have since learned that Mongolians never alter their plans because of weather. Besides rain is a good thing – not something to dread.

Confirmation

Throughout our deputation we showed a video of the 1998 visit. On it were some Mongolian Christians songs. One song I probably heard 50 times or more during our presentation. On the bus while riding through a lush green valley with the rain coming down, they began to sing that same song and my heart just filled to overflowing with joy. What an overwhelming confirmation that I had finally made it to Mongolia - the land of our calling!

I want to talk!!!

We had songs and preaching on the bus and then went into a small cabin where they served food. We went out into a field for games – capture the flag, football (despite the meadow muffins) and dodge ball (while also dodging the aforementioned meadow muffins).

Some local children gathered around us. Beautiful engaging children! We communicated without words. They stole our hearts immediately. I never itched to teach Sunday School so bad in my whole life! I tried my limited Mongolian on one little girl by asking her name. She told me and then started chattering. Dogi had to rescue me!

I wished we could just push a button and know a new language! I wanted so desperately to communicate with these people! I prayed the first of many, many prayers that God would help me learn the language! Charlotte and I learned our first Mongolian Christian song from Dogi. Charlotte could even harmonize. What fun!

We went back inside the cabin for songs and testimonies. Dennis preached with Egi translating and then the pastor also preached. It hailed while we were inside. It was the biggest hail I've ever seen and it bounced several inches off the ground. We went back up the hill (3/4 mile – pretty steep incline) for a Bible quiz and to take pictures. There was no more rain but the wind was very cool. Obviously our blood is not as thick as theirs yet! The fellowship was sweet even though we had language difficulties. Salvation shows in the eyes – with life and hope communicated without words.

Back at our hotel we learned that the restaurant was still closed so dinner was the same as lunch - bread, cheese, nuts, cookies and hot tea! We made the tea in a glass since we had no cups. I stirred the sugar with the blade of my Swiss Army knife. Necessity is the mother of invention!

The water had been turned back on and a shower felt wonderful. We then drew water in case we had no water the next morning. You don't have to shoot us in the foot twice! Now we always keep water on hand for when the water goes off. That's just life in Mongolia.

Our first Mongolian worship service was fantastic! How can such a foreign place feel so comfortable? Only God can do that! It was overwhelming.

Home Where I Belong!

August 1999
We are here!

The following writing was sent to our friends and subsequently published in a missionary publication. It is a summary of our arrival in Mongolia.

We are in Mongolia! The first few days, it seemed like we were in a fog – like it wasn't really real after waiting so long and talking about it and planning for it and traveling for over a week to get here. But now we have settled into our new home – and as testament of God's amazing grace – it truly does feel like home! What other explanation could there be for feeling so comfortable in such a strange place?

Living in a developing country certainly teaches a person patience. Nothing is uniform. Things don't work consistently. Our apartment has two different kinds of electrical plugs and only some of them work and a plug that worked yesterday may not work today. Today you have water. Tomorrow morning, you may not. Conducting business would be time-consuming even if we were fluent in the language. Couple that with the language/translation issue and you feel productive if you accomplish two things in one day! So please keep that in mind when I tell you all that God helped us to accomplish in one short week.

We got all of our luggage here. Sounds like no big deal, but the next time you move a pile of Action Packers through two countries, tell me how easy it is.

We opened bank accounts and it only took a couple hours!

We registered at the U.S. Embassy. We opened a Post Office Box and it only took three trips to the Post Office to do that!

We signed up for Internet service, obtained the proper phone connector (after walking several miles from store to store) and I finally got the thing working.

We located and registered in a language school. They are getting us a one-year student visa.

We found two apartments in the same building and moved into them. We have been cleaning, unpacking and setting up housekeeping this week. We start school next week. You may wonder why it takes an entire week to settle into an apartment. Well, I can't even begin to describe the condition of the apartment. It has given new meaning to the word "crud". Hal and I scraped it with a knife, scratched with a scratcher, wiped it with rags and then disinfected the whole thing one more time! Our apartment now smells halfway decent. It will never be this clean again – but it will be my dirt then.

We are very pleased with the apartment we found. It is fully furnished, in a good location and is very light with one side getting the morning light and the other side getting the afternoon light. We were told it is a warm building – meaning good heating in winter, but I have a gut feeling that was the owner trying to rent an apartment to dumb Yankees. We have two decks with clotheslines.

We have found Action Packers to be multi-purpose objects. After getting our belongings here, they are now serving as: end tables in the living room (with cloths adding to the décor), a nightstand in the bedroom, turned on end – one is a cupboard for folded clothes and one is a printer stand. One is serving as our safe and the others just grace the extra bedroom.

We are buying dishes, pans, silverware, trash cans, etc. plus stocking basics in the kitchen (flour, sugar, rice). Everything is purchased downtown and carried home either on a crowded bus or taxi. I was so proud yesterday because I got home with six eggs unbroken – on a crowded bus. By the way, eggs are sold loose – no cartons, but I cheated and bought a plastic egg carrier. I still worried on the bus because if Mongolians want to get by you, they don't say anything. They simply put their shoulder into your back or side or front or whatever and move you out of the way. Move me – but don't touch my eggs!

August is the wettest month in Mongolia. We have had rain over half the days we have been here. You can tell that it will get nippy real fast. We have worn sweaters on several days and every night we sleep under the quilt our church family gave us! What a joy and comfort to see all those names and greetings on the quilt. So much love is represented by that quilt. The first morning I got up and starting crying every time I looked at a different family square. I had a lot of work to do, so I quit looking. But now I can read the names and greetings and scripture verses and not even cry … much!

Home Where I Belong!

Food supplies are good. There is far more fresh fruit and vegetables than Hal saw last year. We have visited several markets (groups of vendors) and we find almost anything you could ask for. We see many familiar products even though the labels may be in Mongolian, Chinese, Russian or German.

The most exciting part of all this is not the physical stuff we have accomplished, but the thrill of living by faith. I have never had the opportunity to live this way. God has always provided the means for me to take care of myself through work. I have never had occasion to be totally dependent. I'm not bragging. I'm not complaining. I am stating fact.

Every day we are facing things that we cannot possibly control ourselves. We start each day having no idea where it will lead. Charlotte likened it to being on a high cliff and stepping out into thin air and suddenly God's hand is under your feet – solid, reliable, sure. But then the next day, you once again step into thin air and even though you know God was there yesterday and you believe He will be here today – you never quite get over the breathtaking thrill of having absolutely no idea where you are going or what you are doing, but God is there – solid, reliable, sure. What a mighty God we serve!

Rick Shelton and The Way recorded a song that fits our lives right now. Part of it is:

> I'm trusting in the Unseen Hand
> That guides me through this weary land.
> And some sweet day, I'll reach that strand.
> Still guided by the Unseen Hand.

I have talked about faith, studied faith, taught about faith, desired faith and on occasion even exercised some faith (obviously – I am saved and that takes faith), but I have never in my entire life lived each day by faith like we are living now. I recommend it highly!

And now I'm settling into a place that is about as foreign as you can get. Yet as strange as it appears to my eyes and nose, my heart feels at home! Incredible!

You can't really describe this place. You have to experience it! We long for the day we can communicate with these people who have suffered so many years of oppression. Yet we have met with Mongolian Christians whose faces literally shine with the joy of the Lord! It is a unique experience to face someone with whom you cannot communicate a single word – yet you feel the mutual love of God.

I'll close with a huge thank you to all of you who are praying for us. We literally feel those prayers! We were sent off with so much love and support and we desire to do a good job over here. All four of us feel so honored to be on this team and to have a part in this exciting ministry! Thank you to all of you and please keep up the prayers. Our next challenge is a long, hard one – learning the language. Please pray that all of us will be able to do this and do it as quickly as possible.

Love, Jenny

Chapter 5

TO THE ENDS OF THE EARTH!

...all the ends of the earth have seen the salvation of our God.
Psalm 98:3b

When I was a little girl, if my mother wanted to refer to a place that was very far away, it was always "Outer Mongolia". That's all I knew about Mongolia until 1998. As it turns out, my mother was not alone. Other nations have called Mongolia "the ends of the earth" for centuries! Maybe it's because it is so big or because it is so sparsely populated. Or maybe it's because.....it really is the ends of the earth!

The Bible says this place will see the salvation of our God. Even though Mongolia has embraced Buddhism for centuries. Even though they were prevented from hearing the gospel and became atheistic under 70 years of socialism. Even though their language simply doesn't have some words needed to describe spiritual matters. Despite all these things, the Bible says Mongolia too will see the salvation of our God. And we believe that!

Late August 1999
Getting Settled

We pushed hard to get all our household tasks done in one week before school began. Computer and email access was on the top of my list. Of course, that did not go without problems, but tenacity paid off. Every day we walked downtown to buy things we needed. When we had all we could carry, we came home.

We got the things we needed to survive: an iron, cereal bowls, a cutting board, clothes pins, pillows….just stuff. We needed a new stove because the one that came with the apartment had two burners with settings of On and Off. The landlady left a rice cooker which I used for everything under the sun. One day it "roasted" a piece of chicken.

Our First Pot Bless

The pastor of our sponsoring church says that there is no such thing as luck where God is concerned, so Christians should have Pot Bless instead of Pot Luck. The first week Charlotte and I had our first Mongolian Pot Bless.

We coordinated stuff since neither of our kitchens is big. (My kitchen has no counters. I fix meals in midair and store everything on one shelf.) I carried my rice cooker to Charlotte's and fixed spaghetti in it. There was no plug in the kitchen so we put it on Dennis' night stand in the bedroom. It only dribbled on his side of the bed a little bit. We learned new levels of flexibility!

Our dinner was good. Charlotte fixed the sauce using a jar of spaghetti sauce and mushrooms. I attempted garlic bread by using Door Stop Bread (that is what we call the local round loaves. You can guess why we call them that.) I smashed some fresh garlic into soft butter and spread it on the bread and fried it in my skillet. Not bad. Charlotte even found some real lettuce and salad dressing. We felt soooo American – errr I mean Italian! It was fun. We washed dishes and sang. Two altos harmonizing! That was beautiful!

Help! I'm in prison!

Hal started the routine of going over to Dennis' apartment every afternoon – joining Dennis in a two-hour Bible study with Egi. I enjoyed my time alone as I slowly adjusted to having a full-time husband underfoot – along with all the other adjustments of course!

I was the typical independent American woman. In this developing country, Hal felt protective of me and insisted on going with me everywhere! This sounds sweet but after a few weeks I felt like a prisoner – either locked in my apartment or "chained" to Hal. One day, fearing for my sanity, I declared my freedom. I took a little money and went to the market near our apartment – by myself! Just walked around. Didn't even buy anything. I just needed to get out on my own for a few minutes.

Now I go lots of places by myself. Sometimes I walk, sometimes I go by bus or by taxi.

Parting of the Mutton

We visited Darkhan when we first arrived. We were bouncing along a pot-holed road with dirt blowing in our faces. Up ahead we saw a flock of sheep crossing the road. Our driver (who made Hal's driving seem downright calm) started honking his horn and only slowed down a little. The poor sheep didn't know what to do. We went right through them. We could hear them bumping into the van. We squealed and covered our eyes. Charlotte commented that it was the "parting of the mutton" – and that is what it looked like! One sheep was hit but was able to limp away. The driver opened his door and looked back to be sure the sheep could walk and then kept going.

God Directs Our Paths

One Saturday evening about two weeks after we moved into our apartment there was a knock at the door. We heard a woman's voice speaking English. We opened the door cautiously. (Maybe the English-speaking woman was a front for a big, mean man.) All we saw was a petite sweet lady – our next door neighbor. She asked to use our phone because hers was out of order. She asked about who we were and what we were doing in Mongolia. When she learned that we were Christians, she shared with us that she and her daughter both knew Christ as Savior. She immediately asked us to pray for her husband and son who were not Christians.

Thus we met Dema – the precious neighbor God placed into our lives. We were just beginning to understand why our apartment felt "right" when none of the others did.

Warm Chocolate Cake

A few weeks after we got here, we had Dennis and Charlotte over for refreshments. I stirred up a simple chocolate cake (from scratch of course) and sprinkled it with powdered sugar. I served it warm. Either that was a delicious cake or we had been away from home a while! Simple pleasures – enjoyed more than ever!

Questions Men Ask and other Assorted Things

When we came to Mongolia, Mom (at a very tender age) learned to use a computer for the first time. Oh the things mothers will do to stay in touch with their children! Because all of my writing about Mongolia was about girlie stuff (excuse me but that's the only view of life that I have), Daddy even got on the computer to ask his questions. Here are the answers.

Trucks: There are actually more trucks than I expected. Hal says last year they saw very few pieces of equipment. Everything was mostly done by manual labor. Now there are several cranes operating around construction sites in town. There are some large trucks but no semi's. There is about 600 miles of highway and it is mostly around Ulaanbaatar. So there is no interstate commerce like in the states. Most things come in on the train – either from China or Russia.

Tires: Once we were walking by a big parked truck and noticed that the rubber tread had peeled off the tire. They had patched it using a thin metal plate and nails! No kidding! I've never seen anything like it before!

Construction here is truly amazing. It is the sloppiest workmanship I have ever seen in my life! Nothing is square or straight and absolutely nothing is finished off by American standards. Since the buildings are all concrete or brick, all pipes and electrical wiring is on the wall – not covered by anything. Their brickwork is pitiful. They use mostly sand and water with only a little cement in the mix. Then they slop it on and never finish the mortar "seam" so mortar (such as it is) just oozes out from between the brick. There is some granite and marble work and it is fairly nice – mainly because they jam the pieces together.

Look out! At construction sites (and there is a lot going on), there is no protection or barrier or anything. OSHA would have a cow over here! The cranes are setting on hunks of cement or boards – and they don't look stable and are seldom level. Then the hook they use (usually to hoist up pallets of bricks) is an open J hook. No latch. No second hook. Nothing. One Sunday we were walking to lunch and I happened to look up to see a pallet of bricks being hoisted up. I was square under the brick. I ran. No, it didn't fall, but I felt better out from under it.

Walking here is dangerous. There is no other word for it. You can't walk along and look at the sights. You have to look down all the time. There is very little concrete sidewalk. Most sidewalks are squares of concrete blocks with dirt in between. But some of the squares teeter-totter and you never know until you step on them whether it is going to teeter, totter or be stable. So you always have to be prepared for a little ride.

Then there are major gapping holes, open trenches, mud puddles, garbage, human and animal feces, grass, lots of broken bottles with jagged edges of glass sticking up. Occasionally there will be a stretch of sidewalk with regular flat concrete. But you better not relax. Invariably there will be metal pipes sticking up – sometimes a few inches – sometimes more. Of course, there is no warning or barrier or anything. Often there are coils of wire or jagged metal flopped across the path just waiting to snag your pants – or worse yet – your skin.

As you walk, you accidentally kick rocks (because the place is very rocky) and that isn't so bad, but you have to be careful because if you kick the rock forward, you might stumble over a rolling rock in front of you! (As if there aren't enough obstacles in the way.)

Stairs are exciting and there are lots of stairs to climb in Ulaanbaatar. None of them have handrails. Our apartment is on the third floor. The elevator runs from the fourth floor up so we always take the stairs. Often steps vary in depth. So as you are going down some steps, the first one might have a six inch rise, the second one a six inch rise, the third one a six inch rise and in case you think you have a rhythm down, the fourth one will be a three inch rise which jolts you awake in time for the fifth step which might be a 15 inch rise!

Thresholds are a whole 'nother story. There are no flat thresholds in this country. We have read that Buddhists believe evil spirits travel along the floor so by putting a raised threshold of several inches, they are deterring evil spirits from entering. Every doorway has a piece across the floor. That piece might be two inches or 12 inches. You never know. Don't be fooled by what looks like a flat threshold with carpet over it. The carpet is just lying on top of the raised threshold and if you aren't careful, the change in elevation will trip you.

So the key is to pay attention when you're walking – I mean besides being aware of your surroundings so you don't become a victim of pickpocketing. But with all of this – we walk three to five miles a day. We are feeling very in shape. I think I could do the walking with no problem, but usually the last couple of miles, we are lugging stuff from the store so we figure those miles must count double!

Blankets: This week we bought a camel hair blanket. Oh my goodness! It is so warm and soft. Not as soft as cashmere but far less expensive. So I feel better prepared for winter.

Radiators: We are learning that September is a difficult month because the weather is changeable and the radiators are not turned on until middle of the month. They turn the heat on (in every apartment all over town) at about the same time. It makes no difference what the temperature is. They do it by the calendar. My living room furniture is extremely uncomfortable so I bought blankets for the couch and two chairs. It gives a little padding between your behind and the 2x4. I have one blanket on our bed but if it gets really cold, the couch will lose its blanket to go on our bed.

Occasionally I do what I call silly writing. Here is one such composition.

Bubba Gets a New Assignment
Heaven – Early 1999

Setting: God entering the Guardian Angel Division of Heaven to discuss a new assignment with Bubba, Division Supervisor.

God: Hey, Bubba, how's it goin? Stayin' busy?

Bubba: As always. Somewhere in the world someone is always needing protection. You know my division is on call 24 hours a day.

God: Yea, well I have a new assignment to add to your list. A team of four is going to Mongolia in July and I need you to cover them for me.

Bubba: So I can properly staff this assignment, is it going to be short-term or long-term?

God: The guys did the short-term thing last summer.

Bubba: Oh yea. I remember. Two weeks. My troops did a really good job. They didn't even get an upset stomach.

God: Well now two of the men are returning with their wives for a long-term assignment. Dennis is the missionary.

Bubba: I remember him! It just so happens that the troop of angels who protected him when he served in Vietnam is coming off another assignment. I'll reassign them to Dennis. It will be good for them to see that their work in Vietnam has paid off. Dennis is a fine preacher and now he's going to be a missionary! Besides my men deserve a cushy assignment now and then. Guarding an unsaved person through the ravages of war in Vietnam is not an easy assignment but my staff did their usual fine job. Watching over a missionary in Mongolia will be a "walk through the clouds" for them! And I presume Charlotte, his wife, is going?

To the Ends of the Earth!

God: That's correct.

Bubba: My records show our last major assignment for her was for a troop of "health" guardian angels back a few years ago when she had cancer. I'll reassign them to her and add a few for miscellaneous coverage. She will need some "emotional" guardian angels because leaving that new grandbaby is not going to be easy for her. You know, God, I prefer to overstaff assignments rather than overwork my angels.

Bubba: So who are the other two on the team?

God: A couple by the name of Harold and Jennifer Johnson.

Bubba: A systems analyst and a law firm administrator? That's strange. You usually send preachers to mission fields, but hey – you're the boss. I just dispatch protection to those you say.

Bubba: Wait a minute. This is good for staffing purposes. We have had a large group of angels protecting Hal for years. He drives like a bat out of …… well, you know God, he drives really fast! It has been keeping some of my best men busy for years. I can give them a little vacation now because I see from your notes that this team will be walking everywhere they go. God, I really appreciate it when you make changes like this that help me. Do we have any Christian racecar drivers? I could reassign Harold's angels there. They are fully trained.

Bubba: Now this Jennifer person. Haven't had any special requests according to our records. I do see that everytime we turn around, she is putting in another request to watch over her children. They are not bad kids. They just do the normal things, but honestly, this woman is so tenacious. Everyday. Everyday. She even prays for daughter-in-laws before she even knows who they are! Yes, she is a strange one. I see from my notes that she is a little clumsy so I'll have to dispatch a few extra "walking" angels to help her escape the broken concrete, holes, rocks and slippery ice in Mongolia.

Bubba (mumbling to himself): Why does it seem He always sends the clumsy ones to places like Mongolia! Doesn't He have any sure-footed Christians He could send? And this woman is tagging along with a man who is not even an ordained preacher! What is the world coming to? An end, I guess.

Bubba (addressing God respectfully): OK. I'll get this covered and keep these folks safe until you change their assignment. Is that all?

God: Well, for now. Others will be going to Mongolia as soon as I finish my work on their hearts. I'll keep you informed. Keep up the good work!

September 13, 1999
The Desires of the Heart

Delight thyself also in the Lord; and he shall give thee the desires of thine heart. Psalm 37:4

You will notice that this verse does not say your desires must be big, grand, noble desires or even highly spiritual desires - like winning souls. It merely says "desires".

From the day I began music lessons (41 years before we came to Mongolia) I had never gone more than a week or so without being near a keyboard of some kind – piano being my keyboard of choice. That is until we moved to Mongolia. I went six weeks without touching a piano! That may sound like a silly thing, but God knows me and He knows that I worship at a keyboard. I don't play beautifully, but it is an expression from my heart. And oh how I missed it!

A church owned the building where our language school was located. I saw a piano in a room with a glass door and I drooled. The room was always locked and in addition, the piano was locked. I asked the lady at the front desk about playing that piano. I was told I could play it if I paid. Money was a very small price to pay to get to play again.

She sent me to the old man in charge of the keys. He sent me to the lady who cleaned the bathrooms. She sent me back to the lady at the front desk. Mongolians hate to tell you no. So they don't. They send you here and there and hum and haw and make excuses, but they never tell you no. I was definitely getting the Mongolian Run-Around. But in the process of doing that, the guard (in gestures and sign language) said that the key to the piano was hidden in the bench. That would prove to be very valuable information.

I prayed that I would gain access to a piano and I asked others to pray for this silly little request of mine. Then one Monday morning we arrived at school about half an hour early. I told Charlotte I was going to go check the room. It was unlocked!!! I didn't waste a single minute to go back and tell Charlotte or even to turn the light on. I quickly found the key to the piano (right where the guard said it was) and sat down and began to play for the first time in six weeks. Charlotte heard the familiar melodies and joined me. We expected the guard to come and run us out of the room, but in a few minutes he came in smiling and turned on the lights for us!

The joy of touching a keyboard washed over me as I played songs from memory. Charlotte and I sang in our harmonizing alto voices and then we had a good cry and a hug. God cares about us so much to give us the desires of our heart!

I learned that the guard would often "forget" to lock the room on Sunday evenings after their services so I could begin my week with a few minutes at the keyboard. In the Spring of 2000 the church moved and took the piano with them, but by then I was weaned from my need for a keyboard. God knew I had given up a lot in a short time and that I couldn't go cold turkey with the piano. So He provided a little bridge between touching a piano everyday and going from furlough to furlough without playing. Thank you Lord!

So I closed my weekly writing that week with: Continuing to enjoy this exciting journey and God's awesome blessings in this faraway place! How blessed I am! Privileged among women! Thank you for praying for us - for big and small things!

Soon and Very Soon

Once in class we were playing the Memory Game. There was

one pile of slips of Mongolian words and another pile with English words. We had to find matches (and of course say the Mongolian word). Without any prior discussion and having never shared the song before, one of the other Christians in the class picked up the English word "soon" and while reaching for the Mongolian pile of words began to sing "Soon and very soon, we are going to see the King". And all of us joined in immediately. Our teacher just stood there amazed. It was a special moment!

Would you please act the part?

One morning during break for some reason we were feeling silly. Maybe it was too many hours studying Mongolian suffixes. Charlotte began to do a crazy moonwalking thing across the floor. I tried to copy her and couldn't budge. My feet moved like hers but my body didn't go anywhere. Dennis tried it and looked even sillier. Hal (being the dignified one on the team) just shook his head and laughed. I commented that they pay us good money to do this! Dennis replied "Yea, if they saw you now, you would be fired as a missionary." So Charlotte and I tried to put on our "Missouri mule, brow-beaten missionary wife" faces, but we couldn't because we were giggling too hard. It's not our fault that on some days God puts giggles inside us.

Sometimes I think the most important thing I brought with me to this place is my sense of humor. It has helped me more times than I can count! We often say "I don't think missionaries are supposed to be having this much fun." But deep in our hearts we know that God has authorized the fun times just as much as He has permitted the hard times.

Missionaries on their way to a party land in Police Station!
(A title you won't read on any monthly mission report!)

Dennis, Charlotte, Egi, Hal and I were on a bus on a Friday evening on our way to the twins' birthday party. Suddenly Dennis realized that he had just had his pocket picked and lost about 40,000 tugs ($40). He told Egi and pointed out the young boy that he thought had done it.

Egi approached the boy and sternly quizzed him. The young boy innocently displayed his empty shirt and pant pockets. Egi searched him and patted him down pretty good. For a while I thought sure Dennis had misidentified the culprit. Then an older man told Egi that he should check the boy's pants. Egi told him to unzip his pants to which the boy made a rude remark. Egi told him to do it! When he did, the boy carefully held a wad of bills against his waist band over to one side. Egi immediately recovered the money (which was 40,000 tugs) and when the boy tried to escape off the bus, Egi grabbed him.

The bus driver went off the established route and delivered all of us and the man who witnessed him putting the money in his pants – to the police station. The young boy started crying and tried to get away. Egi is a lot stronger than his skinny frame reveals! At one point Hal took Egi's notebook computer case and umbrella and Egi had the kid in a bear hug to control him. Egi doesn't like anyone messing with his foreigners. The witness also said it bugs him when young thugs pick on foreigners so he was glad to help Dennis recover his money.

The young man comes to Ulaanbaatar just to pick pockets and make some money. He was working alone – which is why he was caught. Usually pickpockets work in pairs so they can pass off the money so the one you see take the money never has it on him.

After a considerable delay, we finally made it to the party. Egi even bought the birthday cake he was assigned to bring home. We don't carry money in pockets anymore – other than bus fare.

There's always room for one more!

You can see this next sequence of events almost everyday, but it is different when it happens to you.

Our trolley was unusually crowded that morning – probably because it was the first cold day. We were part of a large crowd to get on an already full bus. Hal and Charlotte got on first and Dennis and I were the very last to get on. I commented to Hal that if I didn't make it on this bus, I'd take the next one. He reminded me that I had no tugs on me! (Now I always have a little money on me when I go out even if I am going with Hal.) So I stepped on the step as the driver began to roll. They do that a lot. You have to be prepared to jump on a moving bus!

First, I felt the step give under my weight. It was an old trolley and the step had worn out and been replaced with old lumber that didn't feel stable. So we rolled for several hundred yards with the door open and my behind hanging outside the bus. Dennis was in a similar position in the other half of the door. I had on gloves which made my grip slide on the rounded steel handrail. Then the driver hit the button to close the door. None of the people in the bus had moved enough for me to get inside. I thought maybe the door would stop when it hit a solid object (my behind), but it didn't. I think I lost part of my right cheek. But it definitely motivated me to shove the person ahead of me – which happened to be Hal. That pushed him into the person in front of him, etc. If I had had a free hand, I would have reached through the crowd and goosed a few people.

Anyway, at the first stop people wanted off. I wasn't about to step off the bus for fear I would never get back on. So I stood my ground.....well my trolley step. The person getting off shoved me so that my body was draped over the handrail into Dennis. (I was thankful it was Dennis I was plastered against instead of a smelly herdsmen.) But it eased up enough that I was able to shove into the aisle and get off the step and out of the door. Thankfully.

Please excuse the rewrite of this gospel song:

> There's room on the bus for me.
> There's room on the bus for me.
> Though millions have come, there's still room for one.
> There's room on the bus for me.

Random Thought

This place could try the patience of a saint....and I'm no saint.

Revelation

Yes, we had hard days – lest you think we were on a constant high. All of us hit rock bottom at times. We decided we needed a code word for when one of us was getting near the edge. We chose "Revelation" - the end is in sight. It meant that person needed to have some slack for whatever reason.

Culture shock is strange. For days or weeks you handle everything (like crowded buses, the total confusion of language learning, having to work so hard at simple tasks) and then one day, you feel like you can't handle one minute more. No more! Not one more thing! You have to get away or you will scream.

One day Charlotte walked out of language class for 15 minutes. One day Hal walked out for the rest of that session. I broke down more than once (usually in the toilet room where there was privacy). Dennis got close one day and almost didn't come back to class after break.

Thankfully we didn't all hit the wall at the same time. (A benefit of a team.) It also gave us comic relief. I told Dennis once that I was in the second chapter of Jude. (Yes, I know Jude has only one chapter!) Then he said one day he was through Revelation and through the Concordance and he was in the maps - Paul's Journeys to be specific. Hal said he was even worse off. He was at the back leather cover. Charlotte questioned blankly "What Bible?"

We survived our hard times and bounced back ready for more. We seldom went more than a few days without a good old dose of laughter. Thankfully.

For years I felt sorry for missionaries because they missed so much at the home church. Well, I was wrong! Missionaries may miss a few events back home, but God more than makes up for it – in wonderful, marvelous, knock-your-socks off ways! I'm glad to be here – Revelation Days and all!

October 24, 1999
First Snow – Genesis

Just a normal week. Spent our week fussing with dative endings

To the Ends of the Earth!

on Mongolian words! Trust me - I don't recommend that for you pleasure-seekers!

This morning it was a little overcast and chilly but nothing more. After church we went out for lunch. While we were in the hotel eating, it started to snow. It came down steady for probably two hours. We got to walk in it! I know I will get tired of snow by next April (Afternote: Silly me – actually it snows until May!) but for now, I am really enjoying it. The flakes are the biggest I have ever seen. They look like pieces of cotton floating down from the sky! It is not very cold. Just 28 degrees F. We were just fine except I had to use my scarf for a hat since I didn't take one. I still ended up with white bangs. Hal had totally white hair because he didn't take his hat either.

Egi (with a grin on his face) told us this was "Genesis" - just the beginning! Everything was beautiful with a white blanket of snow. Tomorrow if it is still snowy, I may break out the Big Boots - you know the ones where you feel like a little kid tromping around in Daddy's shoes! They have tread on the bottoms that would make diesel truck tires jealous!

October 31, 1999
Temperature Dropping

Wednesday afternoon Hal and Egi went to the Black Market to get extra folding stools for our Wednesday Night Bible Study. When they left around 2:00 it was 18 degrees F. I literally watched the temperature drop 10 degrees while they were gone a little over an hour!! They were ready for a cup of hot coffee when they returned.

I check our outdoor window thermometer frequently. Here, the temperature is more than just a passing interest. You have to be prepared and dress properly. Of course, the wind makes a big difference.

Thursday morning it was about 5 degrees F when we went to school. During the half mile walk from the trolley to the school, the wind was blowing. I had enough clothes on and was comfortable except for my forehead - the only part of me not covered. First it got numb (couldn't feel it when I touched it with my gloved hand), then it started to ache (sorta like a headache but different). When I got in the school building and got warm, it turned red and itchy. I have now learned to keep all skin covered!

Tonight I noticed the river that runs through town was completely frozen. I found that amazing because it simply did not feel that cold. I was perfectly comfortable - and I even forgot my gloves today! My precious sweet youngest son says I am completely nuts! Nope, my blood has just thickened!

Friday and Saturday our landlord came and sealed our windows and doors for winter. They take strips of foam rubber and twist it tightly and stuff it in the cracks of both sets of windows. (We have double windows and doors.) Then between the two doors out to the decks, they nailed a blanket in addition to sealing the cracks. Boy, it makes a difference! Before he did that, you could feel cold air all around the windows. Now it is warm - except for the natural cold coming from the glass. As part of building maintenance, they changed some heat pipes in the bedroom we use for an office. That should help. Most of the time I still wear a couple of layers of clothes in the house but compared to outside, it is warm.

November 7, 1999
Blessed Assurance

Egi worked with Hal on translating a lesson on salvation. At the end the American author had included the first verse of the song Blessed Assurance. Even though the Mongolians probably won't sing it, Egi insisted that he translate it to include with the lesson. Hal called me in to help.

Egi had translated the word "happy" for "blessed" and the word "guarantee" for "assurance". So it sang "Happy Guarantee, Jesus is Mine" which didn't roll of the tongue to suit me. We finally came up with "Wonderful Confidence, Jesus is Mine". "Oh what a foretaste of glory divine" became "living with Jesus is a sample of heaven". Now every time I sing that song, I will think "Happy Guarantee, Jesus is Mine."

November 14, 1999
Snow and Traffic

Friday night when we went out, it was snowing and the wind was blowing. We took out our down coats for the first wearing. Oh my goodness! I am so glad we brought them. They are warm as toast. The down-filled hood keeps the Mongolian wind away from your neck and head. A good investment for the winter we face!

This morning it was 11 degrees below zero F when we got up at 7:30 a.m. The snow here is very strange. It is like powder - very dry. They sweep it off the sidewalks instead of using a shovel. I think the extremely cold temperature keeps it powdery. I'm sure the ice is here to stay. I am learning how to balance even when my feet slip. I have also learned to walk in snow whenever possible. It gives a reassuring crunch instead of being slippery like ice. There is black ice here where people have walked and it looks like dirt or blacktop but there is really a layer of ice on top.

Yesterday I went downtown on the trolleybus with my next door neighbor. It was really something to watch the buses and trolley. They weren't going very fast but when they put on the brakes, they would slide for several feet on the ice and sometimes their tail ends would fishtail a bit. When we crossed in the crosswalk with the green light on our side, we waited until the cars were completely stopped because even if they are braking for the red light, they might slide through the crosswalk.

Yes, winter certainly brings more excitement and challenges to our lives. The Mongolians take it all in stride. They don't cancel their plans because of what we would call bad weather. It is just normal weather for them. It is actually kind of fun to get outside.

Random Question

Want to know why the ice is slick?
It's because Mongolians blow their nose onto it!

December 5, 1999
Firm Muscles

Nothing exciting here - Praise the Lord! I slipped on the ice many times but never fell completely down. I figure it is part of the overall physical workout. The tension of trying not to slide down on the ice will make for very firm buttocks. I wonder if I walked backwards if I would get a firm tummy. OK. Probably not.

When I start to skate I grab anything or anyone in reach. On Friday that happened to be a Mongolian teenage boy. He prevented me from falling, but the really exciting thing is I immediately told him "sorry" in Mongolian! No delay. No translating in my head. No stuttering to find the right word. It just came out. That means I'm starting to think in Mongolian! You don't know how good that feels after so many weeks of school and so much work and so much prayer!

Hold up my goings in thy paths, that my footsteps slip not.
Psalm 17:5

Just Need a Reminder Sometimes

Just about the time I would almost lose sight of why we were doing this God provided a reminder. Some people may think it is stupid to forget why we were here, but you get so bogged down that you do forget.

One day at church there were two girls about 10 or 11 years old. Cute as could be. One kept looking at me before the service began. I smiled and winked. Her face just burst into a smile. My heart ached for the day I would be able to teach little girls like that about the love of God! They had no classes of any kind for children. When adults are struggling to survive and are new Christians themselves, there is no time for the children – even the children of church members. Many of them leave their children at home. I could hardly wait to begin a ministry with the children. Oh that it could have been that day! But I returned to Mongolian verb tenses to prepare for the day I could teach.

Afternote: Children's ministry began in April 2002 with Mongolians doing the teaching of material I prepared. What a joy to finally see a long-awaited ministry!

I wanted so much to be able to speak more than I could. My tutor told me I am expecting too much too soon. We had been studying for only nine weeks. Unless we were geniuses (which we aren't), we could not possibly be fluent in that length of time. Oh that there were a shortcut!

Maybe all the effort we expended on language study would pay off in souls later on! Every week we requested prayer for our language study.

O death where is thy sting? O grave where is thy victory?
I Corinthians 15:55

Early one morning as I was checking email before going to school, I began to hear some strange mournful music. I figured Hal had turned on CNN and they were running some story from somewhere in the world. Soon Hal yelled for me to come quickly. It was from our corner of the world! And it wasn't on TV! It was outside our window!

A man who lived in our building had died. They keep the dead body in the home until the funeral. They sprinkle spices over the body to control odor and in the winter, they keep a window open for the cold air.

There was a funeral procession right outside. First there was a woman carrying a picture of the deceased man with the frame draped in a blue cloth. Behind her walked another woman with a display board with various medals attached (we assume the honors won by the deceased man). Behind her was an old man in traditional Mongolian dell ringing a bell.

Then came the casket. It was very beautiful – made of highly polished dark wood and decorated with a gold leaf type decoration on top. We noticed the casket was not a true rectangle. It was wider at one end than the other. It was carried by six or eight pallbearers. That is not just an honorary position here in Mongolia like in the States. They actually carried the casket. I presume they had to carry it down the stairs of our building since it would not fit in the tiny elevator. Even if you turned it on end, I don't know if there would be room in the elevator for someone to ride and push the button. So getting it down the stairs must have been difficult.

Behind the casket came a few people (probably family). Then there was a group of 50 or so mourners. In the midst of the mourners was a band composed of two trumpets, two French horns and a drummer beating a bass drum. They played the death march. At the very back was a woman with a container of milk. She used a spoon to sling it into the air.

The procession walked out our entrance, down the sidewalk in front of our building, around the corner and up the backside of our building. There – waiting on the street – was a flatbed truck with wood slats and a line of vehicles including one minibus. The pallbearers carried the casket to the truck and lifted it aboard and then climbed on board with it. The others got in the bus and cars and drove off slowly – with emergency lights flashing.

We hurriedly finished getting ready for school. When we went downstairs, an old woman used a spoon to sling milk into the air all around our entrance. She occasionally would put her hands into a prayer position and say something and then wipe tears from her eyes. Finally the white liquid was all gone and she went back upstairs.

It was a sad way to begin our week but it reminded me of how thankful I was that when we place a loved one in the ground, we are merely disposing of their earthly body. If they knew Christ as Savior, we have a hope to see them again in a far better place.

I Would Love To Tell You

I would love to tell you that this mission we are on is easy, but it's not. Living here is very hard in more ways than I can possibly explain.

I would love to tell you that I absolutely love everything about this place, but I don't. There are things about it that I really don't like very much but God gives me the grace to tolerate those things.

I would love to tell you that I giggle and smile through every single day, but that would be a lie! I have shed more tears that anyone will ever know! It's not my fault Mongolia is a landlocked country! But yes, we do lots of laughing too.

I would love to tell you that we know exactly how we are going to minister to this dry, parched land but we haven't a clue. Everywhere we look there are needs and opportunities. So much to do! So little time until our Lord returns! But for now, we believe we are to study to learn the heart language of the Mongolians! When we finish school we believe God will make it clear where He wants to use us.

I can tell you that God has been faithful in meeting all our needs and a lot of our wants. I feel closer to God than I ever have in my life probably because I have placed more of my life into His hands than ever before – and what an incredible feeling! I feel like I am truly living in the shadow of God.

> *We who dwelleth in the secret place of the most High shall abide under the shadow of the Almighty. I will say of the Lord, He is my refuge and my fortress: my God; in him will I trust. Surely he shall deliver me from the snare of the fowler, and from the noisome pestilence. He shall cover me with his feathers, and under his wings shall I trust. Psalm 91:1-4 with pronouns made personal.*

Thank you Rosie for praying God's feathers around us!

Punishment or Privilege?

I know it is a privilege to be here but sometimes it feels like I am being punished. Father, forgive me for those thoughts.

How many substitutes can you have?

I seldom ever cook anything where I have all the ingredients. We have arbitrarily decided that if you substitute more than half the ingredients in a recipe, you are actually making something new. One missionary who was leaving Mongolia to return to the States to live told his wife that he never wanted her to substitute again. I guess he had had his fill of creative cuisine.

Why?

These are questions burning in my brain. If you ask a Mongolian, they shrug and look at you as if to say "Well, silly! That's the way it has always been!"

The post office has three sets of double doors – for a total of six doors. Why do they only open one door – one single door? That is for people going in and coming out. You can imagine the log jam in that one door – with five doors remaining locked.

In a country where there is six months of winter with constant ice, why do they use marble for flooring which is slick when it is warm and dry and is nothing short of treacherous in winter?

Why are there no handrails on stairs?

Why is every store either five steep steps up or seven steep steps down? Can nothing be built on ground level?

Why do the cars rev their engines while waiting for the light to change? It is like they are gunning for the pedestrians.

Why do the bus drivers for Bus #13 all drive so aggressively? Do they go to a special school to learn to drive that way?

Why do kids stand in the doorway of the bus? Always. And when you try to get off they look at you like you are being the nuisance!

Life's Little Pleasures

Would I have ever learned to appreciate life's little pleasures if I had not come to Mongolia? Things like a cup of hot tea on a cold day. Warm underwear. A hot shower. A warm bed on a cold morning. Green hills after a long winter.

Thieves!

These people are thieves! They are stealing our hearts! One Sunday night after services a young lady looked at me with tears in her eyes and said "thank you for coming to Mongolia". Do you know what that did to me? Just that one simple sentence fed my heart for days...months...years! The minor inconveniences we were enduring suddenly became very unimportant!

Chapter Six

CULTURE SHOCK

When thou passest through the waters, I will be with thee; and through the rivers, they shall not overflow thee: when thou walkest through the fire, thou shalt not be burned; neither shall the flame kindle upon thee. Isaiah 43:2

When the body suffers a severe trauma, it goes into shock. Organs start to shut down in defense. Multiple traumas at the same time cause massive shock. That's what happened to me when we moved here. I had read about culture shock. I had received instruction about it. I seemed to be prepared, but it's like saying you are prepared to have your arm cut off. You can understand theoretically what is going to happen, but can you ever really prepare for the shock of it? I don't think so.

Not one single thing in my life remained the same. Not one!

I left a career that I loved. I was a respected manager and I got a lot of satisfaction from a well-run office. I was one of the founding members of my local professional organization. That gave me a lot of affirmation.

I was a successful homemaker. My home was comfortable and reasonably clean most of the time. I prepared decent meals for my family and entertained successfully on occasion. My husband and I had a long marriage and everything was going smoothly.

To the Ends of the Earth!

I had been active in Boy Scouts. I seldom ever went to the market that I did not bump into a scout (now grown up) or their parents or another scout leader and we could chat and reminisce over the good old days of scouting. Seeing those boys succeed gave me pleasure because I felt I had had a small part in their accomplishment.

I was the mother of two great kids. I was always running into teachers, coaches or other parents and when they asked about my kids, it was so wonderful to share their latest accomplishments. I was so blessed that the boys had stayed out of trouble. Mothering gave me so much pleasure. There was no greater title for me than to be known as "Chris and Craig's Mom".

My ministries at church abounded. I loved leading music with the children each Sunday morning and I played the organ and piano on occasion for worship service. I got to teach and I was active in the ladies auxiliary.

Career, office, staff, home, car, ministries, friends, family, dog, piano – everything was left behind. I moved to a place where I had nothing - not even an identity. Everything was different. Everything was hard. I was a failure at everything. I stumbled when I walked. I couldn't communicate. I couldn't even follow along with the songs at church. Simple things that I had baked since I was a young girl – never turned out right from my Russian oven. I was a bumbling, stupid clutz. My husband was going through his own adjustments. And my body also began to change.

I knew God had called us here. I wanted to be here more than anything. But the body goes into shock with so much emotional and physical trauma.

Often I would come in from language school exhausted and frustrated with my lack of success. After lunch I would lie across our bed and pull the church quilt over me. I just couldn't go on. I couldn't face the three hours of homework or fixing another meal with strange substituted food items and makeshift equipment. I simply couldn't face another challenge!

So I would fall asleep – hurting inside and crying. And several hours later I would wake up in the fetal position – which is not my normal sleeping position. It always surprised me. I knew my pain was real – not just some figment of my imagination. Yes, I knew these were classic signs of depression. Cultural adaptation and depression must be cousins.

And so I would get through each day. Sometimes I felt if I could just vomit that I would get relief from the pain. But I don't puke easily. By bedtime, I couldn't endure another minute of agony and I would fall into bed and beg God to help me go to sleep quickly because that was the only time of day that I was free from pain. Usually I was so exhausted that sleep came quickly. Call it denial or escape. I called it blessed relief from pain.

I laid me down and slept; I awaked; for the Lord sustained me.
Psalm 3:5

Sometimes I couldn't sleep despite the physical and emotional exhaustion. That's when I communed with God at a whole different level. It was not a quick "Now I lay me down to sleep" prayer of a normal person. No. It was the gut-wrenching plea of a person totally overwhelmed with life. The Lord and I just had to get through the pain. And God was always there with me. I found refuge in my Lord.

I am weary with my groaning; all the night make I my bed to swim; I water my couch with my tears. Psalm 6:6

Be merciful unto me, O God, be merciful unto me: for my soul trusteth in thee: yea, in the shadow of thy wings will I make my refuge, until these calamities be overpast. Psalm 57:1

This may not sound like a calamity to you, but it sure felt like it at the time. Sometimes I felt like if I didn't get to see my children, I would die. Plain and simple. The doctors would call it some strange exotic disease but I knew I would die from missing them! It made no difference that they were grown. I had never been away from them more than two weeks in their entire lives. And now I faced two years without seeing them! I honestly didn't think I could do that. And I couldn't – without God's help!

Sometimes the discouragement would get so great that I would begin to wonder if God really called us here. I had the refrigerator magnet that reads "God is too loving to be unkind and too wise to make a mistake." So I must be the exception to that. Why would a God who loves me, call me into a situation that caused so much pain? Why?

And so when I could not stand it any longer, I would go into the back bedroom and close the door and kneel beside the bed. I would stretch my entire upper body across the bed and there I would pour my heart out to God.

Dennis teaches that God knows everything about us anyway so we might as well tell him exactly how we feel. And I did. I would ask "God, are you sure this is where we are supposed to be? Do I really have to endure this?" And each and every time – without fail – God would come along beside me and wrap His loving arms around me and assure me that this was indeed where I belonged. Oh the comfort! Oh the peace! Oh the precious wonderful relationship I found with my Lord! Every single time I would get up out of my prone position – ready to face again my life in Mongolia – with all its pain and difficult adjustments.

Those were such precious times for me, but after a while I began to feel guilty. God had moved in a mighty way getting us to Mongolia and He had blessed us with so much. And here I was going to Him whining about my pain. (Guilt is an easy emotion for me.)

Then one Wednesday night Dennis taught on the last few hours before Christ was crucified - the Garden of Gethsemane. I had heard the lesson and seen pictures of the garden since I was a child. You know the picture – with Christ kneeling so graciously beside a rock, with his head bowed reverently. Not a hair out of place. His hands clasped in that beautiful, artistic form of our Savior praying. I'm sure you know the position I am speaking of.

But that Wednesday night Dennis showed an artist's version of Gethsemane that was totally different. Christ was obviously in agony. No perfectly poised hands. No careful kneeling position. His entire upper body was stretched out across a rock in pain - begging His father. "God, are you sure this is what I'm supposed to do? Do I really have to endure this? But I don't want my will, Father. I want Your will to be done."

Oh my! That was my prayer! That was my posture! Those were my questions! And then I realized that if my Lord went to His father in His moment of agony to get reassurance, why did I think I could get through this pain without the Father's reassurance? Since that time I have never felt guilty when the Lord and I have had a "heart to heart" talk.

I still have those questioning times even to this day. Thankfully they don't come as often as they did in those early days. But one thing for sure – God has never failed to meet me in my hour of need. All I have to do is go to Him. Oh how honored I am to have had the opportunity to get to know my Lord in this way. *But the people that do know their God shall be strong, and do exploits. Daniel 11:32b* Father, are you strengthening me for future exploits?

When my spirit was overwhelmed within me, then thou knewest my path. Psalm 142:3

Our mission trainers gave me counsel by email. Before we came they tried to teach us about the dark valley I was in but valleys are not fully understood until you walk through them. And here is my answer back to them:

November 14, 1999
Dear Lynn and Brenda:

Thought I should at least let you know that I didn't die down in the dark valley of culture shock. Like you instructed, I didn't build a cabin there. I did pitch a tent for a few days, but I never much liked camping out so I moved back to the mountaintop. I have placed your advice in my Bible for the next time I need it. Hopefully, I won't have to bug you every time I get low.

I appreciate so much the help you sent by email. What you said sounded vaguely familiar so I pulled out my binder from mission training and sure enough, I found lots of stuff about culture shock. Now I can say "been there – done that"!

Some people think the worst thing for us is doing without things! Can you imagine?! Things are the least of my worries. I miss my kids!!!! God is being faithful to help me deal with this and my sons and daughter-in-law are growing in faith through this experience. But if I told the folks at home how I was feeling, they would think I was going stark-raving crazy. (That possibility has passed through my head a few times!)

By the way, now I understand why missionaries should sell their houses when they come on the field. If I had had a home to return to, I probably would have been down at the airport getting on a plane, but I didn't have anyplace to go so I stayed here!

Thanks for listening and for being there for us. It is a comfort to know there is someone who understands what we are going through. We continue to feel honored to be a part of spreading the gospel at the ends of the earth!

Sick and Tired

Being on the foreign field is like raising children. You love them more than words can describe but they can also drive you crazy at times. This was written during one of those crazy times.

Today I am tired. Not tired like needing a nap or needing a vacation. Tired as in sick and tired. You know – fed up!

I'm tired of the dirt and grime. I'm tired of having to step over big globs of phlegm on the ground – and feces. I'm tired of garbage piled around. I'm tired of people blowing their noses into the air and me catching it if I'm walking too closely behind them. I'm tired of the wind almost blowing my head off. I'm tired of aching sinuses. I'm tired of the crowded buses and the pushing and shoving. I'm tired of the musty, mutton smell that is everywhere.

I'm tired of Mongolians laughing at my attempts to speak their language. I never laugh at their butchered English. Why do they feel comfortable making fun of me? I'm tired of the feeling that I will never be fluent in this language.

I'm tired of everything being hard to do. Everything! I'm tired of stuff always breaking down or not working right. I'm tired of no television in English. Is it a sin to want to escape into an old Home

Improvement rerun occasionally – or an old movie that is actually in English?

I'm tired of the horrible lighting so I can't even read at night. I think I'm going blind from eye strain. I'm tired of uncomfortable chairs. I'm tired of dodging cars in the street because they always have the right-of-way. I'm tired of never having all the ingredients for anything I try to cook. I'm tired of feeling inadequate for this job. I'm tired of my skin always itching because of the water we have.

I'm tired of pickpockets. No, they didn't get anything this time either. All I had in that pocket was dirty Kleenex. But I'm tired of having to always be on guard. I'm tired of slipping and sliding on the ice.

I love this place and I'm glad you called me here, Lord, but I'm just tired. *Come unto me all ye that labor and are heavy laden, and I will give you rest. Matthew 11:28* Surely that means mental rest as well as physical, doesn't it? Please renew a right spirit within me.

And so I struggled (and continue to struggle) through cultural adaptation. We have been told that no matter how many years we live in a foreign land, we will experience this from time to time. But there are other times, when I feel so cared for.

I have learned that people will always disappoint you. The most wonderful supporting church, the most devoted friend, the most loving family member will eventually let you down because they are human. But there is one who will never fail you! Never!

I am Loved!
The hairs of my head are numbered (like that is important!)

I have always thought it curious that God would bother to number the hairs on my head. What purpose does that serve, pray tell? This task does not take much of God's time for those men whose foreheads are "growing" with each passing year. But I have thick hair. Lots of hairs to be counted. Doesn't God have anything better to do?

But now I understand. It is just an extreme example of how much God is interested in us. Even little unimportant things catch His attention. Oh how I learned this lesson here on the mission field.

Caffeine Free

Because of lumps and a racing heart, I have had to watch my intake of caffeine for years. I stupidly didn't bring any decaffeinated products with me from America. I can get decaf coffee at the market. It is expensive but I only drink one cup each morning so it lasts a long time. But in the winter, a cup of something hot in your hand is part of how you survive each day. It is not a luxury. You really need it – especially after you have been outside. I haven't been able to find decaf tea anywhere – which is what I really like. When we went to Seoul, I found some but it was really expensive. I bought one box and used it sparingly.

My parents have been very attentive to my needs since I have been here. If I even hinted at wanting decaf tea my mother would have gone to the store that day and bought several boxes and sent Daddy to the post office that very day to ship it airmail. But it didn't feel like a need - only a silly desire - so I didn't mention it. It is certainly not something that warranted the ridiculous postal charges to get something here. After all I had decaf coffee! I should be happy with that.

Well, we met some missionaries here who were returning to live in the States. We took them to a farewell dinner and she asked if I wanted the things from her cupboard that no one had claimed yet. Now when I lived in the States if you had asked me if you could empty the dregs of your cupboard on me, I would have been appalled and would have said "no" without hesitation. But here in Mongolia that is like a gold mine! I said "Sure".

They brought a huge box full of all kinds of things - things I could really use and things that cannot be found here in Mongolia. The next morning as I put the items away, I discovered a metal tin of tea. The label said it was Indian tea and when I opened it, on top were two tea bags which smelled like Indian tea. But when I dug deeper I discovered, she had filled the tin with an assortment of other tea bags – and every single one was decaf!!! And deeper in the box of goodies, I found a whole box of decaf tea. Can you believe it?!? And I never told her about my desire for decaf tea. I hadn't told anyone!

God just takes care of everything. He used my friend to take care of me. Sure I could sip hot water in the winter, but now I had tea to sip!!! I have never felt so pampered and cared for in my life! I stood in my kitchen with my hand raised to the Lord who loves me and with tears rolling down my cheeks, I thanked Him. I am loved!

Why should I worry or fret? My God has never failed me yet! He even knows the number of hairs on my head – which isn't nearly as important as decaf tea!

Chapter Seven

OUTSIDE MY COMFORT ZONE

One evening Charlotte and I were with Biaraa and Dema. He had to go by the garage downtown to change cars for a day trip he was taking on Saturday. So we got out of Biaraa's car and climbed up into a Russian military jeep. I was a little turned around so I asked Biaraa where we were going (in my best Mongolian of course) and he replied "Hoofskool". I protested loudly because that is a place on the Russian border that is three long, hard days' drive from Ulaanbaatar! He just laughed!

Charlotte and I were in the backseat discussing the fact that I would be outside my comfort zone working with my new language helper who speaks not one word of English. Then we just cracked up as we realized that we were bouncing around in the back of a Russian jeep - winding our way along the back alleys of Ulaanbaatar - after dark - with a Mongolian driving and we were having a great time! Totally comfortable!

Yea, our comfort zone has certainly changed in the past year! In fact, I am convinced that if I ever get back to my comfort zone – I will most likely be uncomfortable.

It is truly amazing that this faraway place has become so normal for us. And things are changing here so quickly. I'm glad I captured a verbal snapshot of life as it was when we arrived. Like the horse-drawn buggy in America, we will never return to those days.

Food

We have found adequate quantities of food - reasonably priced and the variety much greater than we expected. Beef is lean and tasty. Chicken is tough but eatable with tenderizer. Mutton is mutton. Rice is a staple and is imported from China. Potatoes, carrots and turnips are plentiful and are more flavorful than we had in the States. During the summer a fairly broad selection of fruits and vegetables was available. In the winter the selection diminishes to apples and more apples, potatoes and more potatoes.

Processed or packaged foods (when you can find them) are imported from Russia, China, America and Europe. They are more expensive than the local foods and are frequently past the expiration date, but hey, you'd be surprised how much you will pay for peanut butter or outdated M&M's when you really want them!

There is no McDonald's, KFC, Burger King, Pizza Hut or Denny's in Mongolia. Ulaanbaatar is one of the very few capital cities of the world that is "McDonaldless". Local restaurants try to present American cuisine and if you stay here long enough, it almost tastes like a hamburger!

We didn't come here for the food. We came here to bring the Bread of Life to Mongolians who are starved for basic Bible truths. Oh what a joy to see their eager faces as God's Word is presented! Missing the taste of a good old American hamburger is worth every bit of it! Pray that God will use us to teach this nation as commanded in Matthew 28:19.

Dress

The traditional dress for Mongolians (both men and women) is a wrap-around garment called a "dell". It hangs straight from the shoulders and is belted. Gained a little weight? – no problem. Just don't tie your belt so tight. Pregnant? – no problem. Wear the same dell moving the belt higher.

Dells are usually made of satin imported from China. They are very colorful (men wear darker colors and women brighter colors) with beautiful accent trim and buttons. Summer dells are lined with cotton fabric. Winter dells are lined with sheep fur for warmth. Often the sleeves are very wide at the wrist and hang several inches below the fingertips – for ease in scrunching your arms up into your sleeves in cold weather. Yes, men wear pants under their dells. Women also wear pants or tights in the winter. (You figure out the wind chill factor with 20 degrees below zero F and a north wind from Siberia!)

Young people in the city wear traditional Western clothes. You see Nike, Reebok, Wrangler, Levi and other name brands. Some are genuine and some are cheap knock-offs from China.

Contrasts

Mongolia is a land of extreme contrasts. You can see a man walking down the street in the traditional Mongolian dress that men have worn here for centuries – and he will be carrying a Nike bag! You can see a horse clomping along pulling a cart overflowing with sheep carcasses passing a man in a business suit talking on a cell phone! This country has square, ugly buildings and toothpicks decoratively carved. Mongolia produces the softest cashmere in the world and toilet paper that could sand hardwood!

You see cars that you really wonder how they stay together much less make it down the road – and right behind them will be an immaculate, black Mercedes with a driver chauffeuring some dignitary through town.

The greatest contrast of all is to compare the hopeless eyes set in a lifeless face of so many Mongolians – compared to those whose faces shine with the love of Christ! That contrast is why we are here! Pray that the Lord will use us to make a difference in lives in this place.

Dirt

When we lived in the States, we liked things clean and tidy but we were not fanatics. There were lots of things more important than an immaculate house, but the Health Department never shut us down either. Then God moved us to Mongolia and just one of dozens (hundreds?) of adjustments we have had to make – is becoming accustomed to one of the dirtiest places on the planet.

You get dirty here without doing anything! I know that sounds like something a kid would say to his mother, but it is true! You can get out of the shower scrubbed and clean and put on a clean shirt. One hour later if you examine the collar and cuffs of the shirt, you will find them grimy. Polished shoes look nice for about two steps outside. Often your fingernails look like you have been working in the garden – and all you have done is sat in class.

When you blow your nose, you see what you were breathing. Buses and cars belch out black fumes that would make the environmentalists faint. Trash is not managed well here and with the winds, it gets blown everywhere. The people have never been taught to put litter in a can. When they have a piece of trash, they drop it on the ground wherever they are. If they need to spit (which is frequent with the air pollution), they spit on the ground. (If you are walking down the street behind someone, stay alert!) If they need to blow their nose, it is done into the air – even if they are inside a building. Dusting your house is good for about 20 minutes – maybe. The dirt we pick up in the vacuum is absolutely mind-boggling!

As I see the dirt and grime everywhere, I am reminded of the scripture that says *our righteousnesses are as filthy rags. Isaiah 64:6* Our attempt to do good is more repulsive to God than dirt is to us. Spiritually we need regular and frequent cleansing. In the 51st Psalm David asked God to "create in me a clean heart". Having clean innards is far more important than keeping the outside clean! And that's why we are here...to teach these precious people about the most important cleansing – having our sins washed away. So we have to get a little dirty to share the message of cleansing. So what.

Abraham Didn't Know

Why do I expect God to reveal His plan for us in Mongolia? He didn't even tell Abraham the plan for his life. God just told him: "Leave your country and go to the place I will tell you. I will bless you." Boy, do I identify with Abraham now. I left my country and have gone to the place God told me. And He has blessed abundantly.

But it sure would be nice to know a little more about exactly what we are to do.

God Still Watching Over Us

When we first got here, God's protection and provision was so obvious every single day – directing us to apartments, the school, etc. But then the days settled into a steady routine. We knew God continued to watch over us because we hadn't slipped on the ice or broken any bones and because we hadn't been run down by any cars, but being the forgetful humans we are, we needed a little reminder. We got it in January 2000.

When we first arrived, we went to the police station to register as we were told. They said we did not need to register. OK, so we figured we misunderstood or the rules had changed. We didn't worry about it any more. We proceeded to enroll in school and got our long-term visa through the school. That was in September.

In January we heard again that we must be registered at the Police Station and that there was a penalty for each day we were not registered. So we went again and learned that indeed we were supposed to register within ten days of getting our long-term visa. (They didn't register us the first time we went because we had only a visitor visa.) The penalty for the four of us from ten days after our long-term visa until January 2000 was over $800! We moaned and felt terribly stupid for not following up on this. Then with more checking, they discovered that the school had registered us when they processed our long-term visa. So God was watching out for us (using the school as His instrument) because we don't have enough brains to take care of ourselves!

Thank you Lord once again for your care and provision!

Bibles Arrive

When we arrived here, we discovered there were Mongolian Christians who can read English who wanted a Bible in English. So we put out the request and a church in California took it on as a project. They are a small church and this was one of their first mission projects. They were so amazed when they raised the entire amount in one Sunday! So they made the arrangements to have Bibles shipped from Florida to us.

Now you must understand that technically it is against the law to ship Bibles to Mongolia. So the shipping company listed the contents as "books" and many of us prayed for their safe delivery. They were long over due and we were beginning to wonder if they had been waylaid. Egi was on alert to join us at the post office to help us if there were problems in customs.

Well, the first box of Bibles arrived. Egi "just happened" to be with us that day. It took about 45 minutes to get them but that is normal processing. The box was not opened. No questions were asked. Hal paid the small amount of duty owing and he and Egi - grinning from ear to ear - carried the box out right past the guard.

Extremes

There are so many extremes in this land!

Products seem to either be wimpy and ineffective or else they are industrial strength – potent enough to melt paint off a car bumper!

It is not uncommon for the temperature to drop 20 degrees in an hour! It can be sunny and warm at 2:00 p.m., hailing at 3:00 p.m. and sunny again at 4:00 p.m.

Mongolians will have ten people living in a small ger and there won't be another human being for miles. Crowded yet sparcely populated.

We have been teaching God's Word for months with no visible result. Suddenly we see people responding. Quite a change! What a blessing!

We go for long months with no visitors from the States. Then we have the unparalled thrill of going to the airport to pick up guests. The joy is incredible! Then ten days later we take our guests to the airport – knowing they are returning to friends and family and we are left here facing seemingly endless months of school and winter. The emotional low of a quiet, empty house is beyond description.

All of this makes us so grateful for the steadfast, unchangeable nature of our God! *For thou art my rock and my fortress; therefore for thy name's sake lead me, and guide me. Psalm 31:3* That's what we desire most in this faraway land – the leadership and guidance of our God! Thank you for your prayers on our behalf as we share the unchangeable God with these precious people!

More silly writing but there is truth tucked away in it.

Humility Breakthrough

It was reported today in the New England Journal of Spiritual Medicine that a great research breakthrough has occurred in the field of humility. Pastors, if you have proud church members, here is the solution to your problem.

You may say that none of your church members hold their heads high, nor puff their chests out nor swagger down the aisle like they own the place. But, I ask you. Do you have members who are successfully pursuing careers? Communicating effectively? Caring for their personal needs such as making food purchases and paying their monthly bills? Do you have members who are confident in their understanding of what is happening around them? Well, then those are people who could benefit from this great breakthrough in humility.

Just send them to live on a foreign mission field. Instantly they will become totally incompetent.

1. They will not be able to buy food without pointing and grunting and sniffing and often they still will not have a clue what they are purchasing.
2. They will not be able to complete a simple business transaction without help.
3. They will not be able to communicate with anyone – even small children.
4. They will not be able to listen to the evening news or read a newspaper.
5. They will not be able to cross a street. They probably think they have the right-of-way if there is a green light. They do

– so long as there is no car coming.
6. Drive a car? Forget it. They will barely have the brains to dodge traffic much less drive in traffic!
7. Walk? They are likely to stumble and trip and bumble along.

Yes, just send us those proud, competent, intelligent people and we will reduce them to babbling, bumbling bimbos in just a few short days. But after a few years, we will return to you a person who while they were learning a new language and culture has gained faith to move mountains – because that is what must be moved for a person to make it on the mission field!

McDonald's

Hal never liked McDonald's hamburgers. He would rather do without than eat one. On January 28, 2000 at 9:04 a.m. the Mongolian Mission Team made an official note of the fact that Hal said he wouldn't mind having a McDonald's burger! We think he has been here too long!

March 5, 2000
Spring, Camels, Elevators and Telephones

Another exciting week. Spring, camels, elevators and telephones. You may think I'm goofy, rambling from one subject to another. It's not my fault God puts an interesting mix of things in my week.

It warmed up to the 20's (above zero, that is) this week and we got all excited thinking spring had arrived and then it snowed on Wednesday. Spring is such a flirt and a heartbreaker!

Monday as we walked along the sidewalk on the main street in town, we saw two camels "parked" in front of the post office. I had never been that close to a camel before. I didn't realize they were so big! Just standing there chewing their cud and looking around with major attitude. What an interesting place we now call home - where camels wait outside the post office!

About the time I think I have experienced every strange event - I find something I missed. On Friday afternoon I went to the State Department Store. Now when you hear "department store" you probably think of Macy's or Sears or Penney's. Wrong! Think of an old Woolworth's bargain basement. That is closer to what we have. They have been making improvements but it is still no where near American standard.

Anyway, the store is four stories high. We usually take the stairs. I tried to take the elevator once, but there was no button and the elevator never came so I ended up taking the stairs. Well Friday afternoon I was tired so I thought I'd try the elevator again. This time there were two Mongolian women waiting for the elevator on the first floor. Every few seconds one of them would put her mouth on the crack of the door and say "nig, nig, nig". That's Mongolian for "one". It took me a few seconds to figure out what she was doing. Sure enough, the elevator arrived. The door opened and there sat the elevator operator on the stool - working the buttons. I haven't seen a manually operated elevator in decades and I've never seen one where you call your floor number into the elevator shaft. Sometimes I feel like I have moved back in time.

One other story: Dogi was excited that her family was getting a telephone. I thought they did not have one because it was too expensive. She said in 1990 when they applied for a telephone, their name went on a waiting list because her grandfather fought in the revolution. Their name just came up!! Yep. A ten year wait. All because of her grandfather's beliefs. We have heard about persecution of Mongolians during that time. I thought all of that ended in 1990 when they came out from under socialist rule, but I guess not.

Mad at God

In March 2000 Craig, our youngest son, surrendered to the ministry. Hal and I were very pleased. We missed his first sermon but felt confident we would get a video of it. For reasons I still don't understand, the video camera failed. We did not get to hear him preach until our first furlough – over a year later. That was a wonderful blessing but this writing was about my disappointment at not getting a video and yes I was a bit angry with God.

Why? Am I allowed no pleasures?

Why did the videotape of Craig's first sermon turn out blank? Was that too much to ask – the simple joy of a mother seeing her son's first sermon? I don't understand. It hurts. God, did you know I would take too much pleasure in it? I have given up everything for you and haven't even whined about it (much). I gave up seeing or hearing Craig preach his first sermon in person. So I don't even get a video of it? OK, so I'm thankful I didn't lose my son. I just don't understand why something so simple and inexpensive is not allowed. Was my desire wrong? It's like everything pleasurable is being stripped from my life – bit by bit.

Afternote: I have since repented. I'm not mad at God any more.

In my weekly writing, I included one-liners about what was happening weather-wise. Not meteorologically correct but my version of life on the steppe. It was called:

It's that time of year when...the air is soft - not biting like in winter.

April 9, 2000
Difficult Days

For reasons I still don't understand, I continue to have difficult days. Yes, I'm still searching for whatever lesson God is trying to teach me. On Tuesday, our class went downtown to visit the library. I thought the school bus was outside and would take us back to the school. But I was wrong. The school bus had left. All the other students just went on home because it was noon, but I had a tutor session that afternoon and had left my book bag at school.

So I found myself downtown at 1:00 and my tutor session was at 1:30 - back at the school - across town. I found 200 tugs poked in my jacket pocket and hopped on a bus only to discover it was not the bus I thought it was. When it turned and started going in the opposite direction from the school, I got off at the first stop. With

Outside My Comfort Zone

no more money on me and time running out, I took off at a fast clip. I was so frustrated, I did what any mature adult would do - I cried all the way to school. But to add to the frustration, I had only one tissue in my pocket so I couldn't even cry freely.

When I got to the school, I went into the restroom and without thinking splashed water on my face to help reduce puffy eyes and then remembered that my drying towel was in my book bag - upstairs in the teachers' room. (Asian toilets do not provide toilet paper, hand soap or towels. You have to carry your own.) So I walked in to the teachers' room to get my bag - looking like I don't know what! When they asked what was wrong, I pretended I didn't understand their Mongolian. Hey, most of the time I don't understand so even when I do understand, it is easy to act like I don't!

After my tutor session, I took a minibus home only to discover the route had changed. I stayed on it until it got across town closer to home but I had another healthy walk to get home. No crying this time. All cried out for the day. Yes, I was very glad to get home at last.

Then Friday morning I was getting on a trolley. Some of the bus drivers drive with attitude - taking off real fast and breaking hard. We call that "packing the bus" because all the passengers get readjusted inside. But trolleys are usually calm and slow.

I think the driver of this trolley had just been transferred from a bus and he was mad. While I was still on the step - reaching for the pole, he took off fast and I went to the floor - hitting my arm and putting a nasty bruise on my shin which hit on the next step up. Everyone just looked at me. I sucked up my hurt leg (and my hurt pride) and got to my feet. I reached the pole and hung on with a death grip as the guy ripped down the street.

I had my fare in my hand that had the death grip on the pole. The toll taker was about three seats up the aisle. They like for you to walk to them to give them the fare - thus keeping the back of the bus clear. I know he didn't understand a word I said but some things transcend language barriers. I looked at him and said "If you want this money, come and get it. I've already been on the floor once." He came and took my fare.

Random Question

If April showers bring May flowers, what does April snow bring?

April 16, 2000
Our Little Village

Not much exciting this week. We are thankful for normal though. Saturday evening two of the language classes got together for a little party. As Hal and I were walking along, carrying our portion of the food for the dinner, we saw another missionary couple we know. They honked and waved.

A little ways farther down the street, we met one of the teachers at our school. He was coming from a Bible Study. We chatted with him before walking on to the party. Hal commented, "Have you noticed that we seldom ever go out without seeing someone we know?" This little village of 700,000 people is getting smaller all the time! It is amazing how this has become our home.

April 2000
Worshipping

We had nine people in church this morning. So many times in my life, if there had been nine people at church, I would have come home totally depressed. This morning our hearts sang with joy! We know at least three of the Mongolians are unsaved and they heard the gospel one more time. I am so thankful that worship is a condition of the heart - not based on the number of people in attendance. We raised the roof with our singing of "Joyful Joyful We Adore Thee" in Mongolian!

Every Knee Shall Bow

We visited the Buddhist Temple here in Ulaanbaatar. The Buddha is about three stories high - made of bronze covered with gold - weighing many tons. On the first floor his feet and toes are about at eye level. On the second level (as high as we could go), you are about at his waist. There are huge precious jewels set into the gold. It really can't be described on paper.

People walk around it and pray with folded hands. They light candles and they twirl the prayer wheels which contain Tibetan writings. (The song that includes the line "feel a little prayer wheel turning" never made any sense to me before but now that I live in a country with real prayer wheels, I simply cannot sing the words in that song.)

People buy small family Buddhas to put in a glass case around the big Buddha. In front of the temple, there is a prayer pole which people touch as they pray. There is an incense pot where they pray and then there are boards that look like ironing boards with the end that is toward the temple slightly elevated. Men stretch out prone on the board for a few seconds and then get up and kneel with folded hands. Then stretch out again on the board and get up - repeating that over and over. It made me tired watching them.

Then we visited the area where the lamas live. I walked into a room where probably 25 or more young men (ages 12 - 20) were sitting cross-legged, chanting from Tibetan books. They seemed to be chanting the same thing with variations and counterpoint chants. When we walked in, they looked up but never stopped chanting. A very intriguing sound.

Seeing the big Buddha made be thankful that my God is not housed in a temple. *Thus saith the Lord, The heaven is my throne, and the earth is my footstool. Isaiah 66:1* As intriguing as it was to hear a roomful of young men chanting, it is nothing compared to prayer to the living God. As we walked away from the temple - watching the old men kneeling and stretching out on the prayer boards, I began to hum...and then sing...

>He is Lord, He is Lord.
>He is risen from the dead and He is Lord.
>Every knee shall bow.
>Every tongue confess
>That Jesus Christ is Lord.

We visited the Buddhist temple the day before Resurrection Sunday which just reminded me again that we serve a living God and we are here to tell the Mongolians that they don't have to depend on a hunk of gold or a prayer wheel or a prayer board. They can have a personal relationship with the Lord of the Universe!

On Saturday before Resurrection Sunday we served a buffet here at the apartment. I told the resurrection story to Egi's children in Mongolian using flannelgraph. When Geralt (one of Egi's three-year old twins) saw me get out the whiteboard and cover it with a camel blanket in preparation for the story, her eyes lit up. I know she remembered it from Christmas. The kids quickly gathered in front of the board with very little coaxing and they sat quietly and listened attentively and Tsaamba even nodded his head a few times in agreement. This may not seem like a big deal, but trust me, when you are struggling with a foreign tongue and a child acknowledges that he understands what you are saying - that is a big deal (to me anyway). So the kids understood me. Praise the Lord!

May 7, 2000
Shoutin' Time in Heaven

> It's shoutin' time in heaven.
> A singer once lost is found.
> It's shoutin' time in heaven.
> Salvation has been brought down.

A Mongolian lady has accepted Christ as savior - the first soul saved as a result of our ministry here in Mongolia! Please pray for her.

So it was a good week here in Mongolia. We returned to school with a new commitment to speak this language. To top it off, Hal found Oreo cookies at the downtown market!!! First time we have seen those since we arrived. I'm rationing myself to just four a day so they will last longer and so I won't weigh 400 lbs.

> **It's that time of year when**....it must be spring – the wind (and the dirt and the trash) is blowing!

Track Season

After being here for ten months I thought I had already stumbled across everything that I miss, but this week to my surprise, I discovered something new that I miss. This is the first spring in eight years that we have not been involved in track meets. Chris ran track four years in high school, one year in college and then the following year helped coach his former high school team. Craig participated in track and field events for four years in high school and two years in college. Hal and I missed only a few of those hundreds of events.

This last week we had warm sun, cool breezes, green grass and trees budding and then one day I saw young people in the position like starting blocks – getting ready to run (they don't have starting blocks) and warm, special memories of track meets flooded my mind. Just one more reminder that I have moved to a new section of my life - thankful for my former life but thankful to be here now, doing what I'm doing.

May 21, 2000
Living the Scripture

The most exciting thing that happened this week was on Wednesday night when a young girl asked a question after our Bible Study. She asked how a person can be born again. Wow! That's why we are here! That's the same question Nicodemas asked in the Bible. (*John Chapter 3*) It is like we are living the scripture! What a joy to share the gospel with these precious, hungry people. Just a simple thing like that, makes all the pain and struggle worthwhile.

Daddy Debuts In Mongolia

In language class we are asked to speak (in Mongolian of course) about various topics. In fact the teachers will accept anything we say – so long as it is in Mongolian. We have no life to talk about – just school, homework, school, homework. Not very exciting (even in Mongolian). Sometimes the students get imaginative. Yes, even this predominantly missionary student population has been known to tell a few tales – just to liven up the class a bit.

So last week when Hal was given the Mongolian word for "saw" (the noun - the instrument to cut wood) and was asked to talk about it and he began to talk about music, the teachers thought he was just making it up. He told them his father-in-law makes music with a saw. They didn't believe him. They had never heard of such a thing. So the next day Hal took a video to school of Daddy playing the saw. He showed it at lunch time when all the teachers were in the lounge. They were quite amazed. The next day one of the teachers mentioned it to me in class. So Daddy is now an internationally-known musician! Way ta go, Daddy!

"Lettuce" Eat Salad

We found lettuce at the downtown market for the first time since we arrived. Last night I made chef salad – with almost all the ingredients. Today we had BLT's and actually had the "L". Yum! Yum! (We had been having BTC's bacon, tomato and cucumber) sandwiches.

Found Q-tips

Another accomplishment. A while back Q-tips (well, a cheap imitation of Q-tips) could be found everywhere. We were lulled into thinking this was an item we could pick up whenever we needed them. Wrong! Been looking for almost a week. Found some in a pharmacy today.

After my Mongolian description (wood with cotton) failed, we saw them and pointed and grunted. Then I decided it was time to learn the word. Quite logically, they are called "ear cleaning". So there you have it! Who says Mongolian is difficult?!

No Lap Yaks Please!

We went to the State Circus and had a really good time. We were sitting in the front row. I could have reached out and touched the animals. When the yaks and horses started running around the ring, just one step up and they would have been in our lap, I hoped they were well-trained. (They were.) We were thankful they weren't Lap Yaks. (Dennis' line which I borrowed.) We saw other trained animals, contortionists, musicians and comedians. I understood very little of what was being said, but understood the humor precisely because it was the Charlie Chaplan physical kind of humor that transcends language barriers.

Church: We had a good crowd on Wednesday night and despite the sweltering heat, they had questions about salvation after the lesson. Goes to prove that the hunger of the soul overrides all other physical desires. This morning we had 14 in service. Some who do not know Christ as Savior are attending regularly. What a blessing! How exciting to be here in this place at this time!

Simple Pleasures

We went to an Independence Day Party at the US Embassy on Saturday. There were several hundred people there. The embassy grounds were immaculate. The concrete was smooth and unbroken, the curbs uniform, the grass thick and nice with flowers everywhere. We sat in lawn chairs – the kind with soft plastic straps. I forgot how comfortable those chairs were! Charlotte and I took off our shoes and sat on the grass (real grass!) and petted a friendly dog that wanders around the grounds. Such delicious little pleasures!

They served BBQ hamburgers and hot dogs, American potato salad, homemade chocolate chip cookies and a bag of M&M's that were not even past the expiration date! Soft drinks and ice cream. They had basketball, ping pong, dart games, a cake contest, a live band – everything for a real American 4th of July.

You probably have heard that Elvis is alive and living in Alabama....or Texas.....or wherever he was last seen. Well, I'm here to tell you Elvis is alive in Mongolia! It was so funny to see a Mongolian crooning out "Love me tender, love me dear, never let me go". He didn't have the hip gyrations down. Somebody said he needs to watch some Elvis movies and add that to his act. He did the voice imitation really well.

The flag ceremony was touching - like I've ever gotten through

To the Ends of the Earth!

any flag ceremony without crying! The Mongolian security guards raised the flag and they had been trained in all the proper techniques to do it with respect. The threatening summer storm gave just enough breeze to catch Old Glory beautifully as the National Anthem finished. I've always been patriotic, but everything seems more vivid and intense here – and this was no exception. Like every other American, I get annoyed with how things are in America sometimes, but I can tell you, there is no more beautiful sight than Old Glory flapping in the wind.

Living in a place where the people have more freedom than they did in prior years but still do not have complete freedom – really makes you appreciate America where you are really free to do anything you want. Here in Mongolia we feel like we have the freedom of someone out on parole. We are free to live where they say, do what they say do, etc. Democracy here is so young and fragile – being just ten years old. It makes you appreciate our heritage of 200+ years of freedom.

Have a wonderful 4th of July and remember to be thankful for real freedom.

July 9, 2000
Like a Kid Out of School

Summer time and the livin' is easy. Fish are jumpin' and the cotton is high. Oh, your Daddy's rich and your Mamma's good lookin'. So hush little baby, don't you cry!

School is out for the summer!!!! Yea!!!! Even I - who can describe almost anything on paper - am at a loss for words to describe how wonderful it feels to be out from under the pressure of school. Real good – that's how it feels.

Dennis, Charlotte, Hal and I went out to eat on Friday night to celebrate. It was a beautiful evening and we ate out on the deck of the restaurant. Then just like kids out of school, we walked through an amusement park and decided to ride the ferris wheel. Disneyland it ain't, but it's the best in Mongolia. We could see all over Ulaanbaatar from on top. The creaking only worried us a little bit.

Categorized Bathing

We regularly lose hot water – sometimes for a week at a time. I love things to be organized, categorized and color-coded (if possible). So this provided yet another opportunity for me to do that. Bathing in Mongolia is in four categories:

1. Sponge bath – better than nothing.
2. Glass shower – you make a pail of warm water and set it in the bath tub. Using a glass you pour the water over you. Better than a sponge bath. (Note: Don't use too much soap or you'll be dripping back to the kitchen to heat more water.)
3. Mini-tub bath – you find the three largest pots you have and fill them with water and heat them on the stove (we only have three burners). Also use the coffee water warmer. Pour all of that boiling water in the tub and add cold water until the right temperature. With these huge, deep Russian bath tubs, you will have about one inch of water in which to take a bath. Refer to Note in #2 above regarding the use of soap.
4. Warm shower – we have a faint recollection of that. The cold water here is so cold, it often hurts your teeth. On occasion when suddenly the hot water has gone off in the middle of a shower, it literally takes my breath away, it's so cold. (Hal says it only borrows your breath!)

Just Came to Love Us

Our first summer in Mongolia, our dear friend Anne came to see us along with her sister-in-law Verla. Anne and I have shared so many things – church work, births, childraising, weddings and funerals. And she is the one who opened her home to us the three months we were homeless before coming to Mongolia. She came to Mongolia for one – and only one purpose – to love us. And that she did!

We spent the week visiting and laughing and crying and visiting some more. As my kids say – Anne and I have never run out of anything to talk about – and it's been this way for 23+ years! We showed Anne and Verla all the interesting places of Ulaanbaatar which didn't take long! We walked around town, went to the Buddhist Temple, went to the Black Market, went shopping and to lunch with Charlotte, cooled our feet in the river, sat in a ger and drove out to the countryside.

Perfectly Safe

Our trip to the countryside turned into an adventure when the car broke down and we three ladies took a bus back to town while Hal and Egi dealt with the car problem. As we bounced along in a hot, dusty, rattletrap of a bus – several miles from town – and I wasn't absolutely certain where we connected with the trolley line which would get us home – and we were the only Caucasians on the bus – and we were dependent on my limited Mongolian – Anne commented "You know, I feel perfectly safe – even now." And we were perfectly safe. We made it home just fine. Made a little friend on the bus – a 13 year old girl that Anne wanted to talk to so badly, she could taste it. Now Anne understands the frustration of living in a place where you can't communicate.

Country Bumpkin Gone To Town

Anne, Verla, Hal and I flew to Beijing for four days. What a wonderful break that Anne provided for us. When we came through Beijing on our way to Mongolia, I thought it was such a backward, developing country (and it is). But this week, I felt like a country bumpkin gone to town!! It was so clean and nice and modern. Honest! Maybe we better plan a trip through a partially developed country when we return to the States – or else we might go into shock!

We stayed at a wonderful hotel that had a drug store and grocery store in the complex in addition to several restaurants. We found lots of things at the grocery story: Crisco, corn starch, Pace Picante Sauce, M&M's that were not outdated, crackers and the best thing – milk! The first night there, Hal came up to me in the market with a big grin on his face and a twinkle in his eye and said "Guess what they have!!!??? Milk!!!" We bought regular milk and skim milk and mixed them and it tasted almost exactly like 2% which is what we drank in the States. So every night we had milk before we went to bed! Yum!!

We visited Tiananmen Square (a very sad place to me – the place where hope of democracy died), the Forbidden City and walked on the wall again. We girls also rode a camel and got a picture to prove it. I must say a camel is more comfortable than a horse. We were wedged between the two humps so we felt very secure and snug. OK, so some of us were more snug than others, but the camel seemed to manage.

The smog was the worst I have ever seen anywhere. It was about 100 degrees and listed on CNN as 100% humidity. No, it wasn't raining. It felt like a sauna. Near the Great Wall, the vendors have colored plastic awnings to provide shade. Drops of water were dripping off the plastic – from the humidity! We bought bottles of frozen water. Delicious! Most of the taxis we took were air-conditioned which was wonderful.

Hal achieved the amazing feat of out-shopping Anne – the Queen of Shopping! After a full day at one shopping area, we went to the hotel to rest before dinner, but Hal went out for another hour and came to dinner proudly displaying his finds.

Reconfirmation of Where We Belong

After an extremely difficult goodbye, we returned to beautiful Mongolia. It had rained so the sky was brilliant blue with white puffy clouds and the hills were deep green. What a beautiful place we call home. As backward as it is here, I am thankful God called us here instead of to China. When we were in Beijing, I looked at the masses of people and of course, I long for all of them to accept Christ as Savior. It was a general desire - different than the specific desire I have for the people of Mongolia – the land of my calling. So the trip was a reconfirmation that God wants us here for now.

We also visited Seoul that first summer. Saw the DMZ, ate Baskin Robbins ice cream and pizza and drank a $5 tiny cup of instant coffee! So our traveling was over. It had been a full year since we had been anywhere overnight. I can't remember ever staying at home that long before. Even as a child, we went to visit my grandparents a couple times a year. Now I was facing another full year at home. Glad to be back to familiar surroundings and clean air. Praying God gives us the grace to get through another year.

The container is never empty.

The widow in I Kings 17:10-16 went to her grain bin and oil container every day and it was always full. You may think such miraculous things don't occur anymore. I tell you they do. Everyday I go to my laundry basket (actually an Action Packer recycled as a laundry basket) and no matter how much I wash or how often I wash, there are always more dirty clothes there! Yes, we wear clothes more than one day, but since a load of clothes – limited by the size of the washing machine tub and the line space I have – is very small and sometimes it takes a long time to get a load dry and then sometimes, we have no water. So it's really a never-ending job. And we don't have children!!

VIP

I have never before lived in a capital city. This is probably common in all capitals but a first experience for me.

Often as we walk around Ulaanbaatar, we see an increased number of policemen and we hear sirens. All traffic stops. Cars and buses pull to the side of the road. The street that was jam-packed a few seconds earlier is cleared of all traffic. There are no exceptions. No business is so urgent as to allow passage. Pedestrians turn in curiosity to see what is coming. It is always some government official or visiting dignitary.

First there is the lead car driving in the point position. Then there is the main car - always an immaculate black Mercedes or other expensive vehicle with government flags mounted on the front. That car is followed by another guard car in the rear. They usually make their way to the Parliament Building in the center of town.

The hustle and bustle of life in the city stops and whatever else was going on is forgotten or ignored when the very important person comes. When I see this, I am always reminded of the day when Christ will return. All life as we know it will stop, but it will never return to normal again.

In a moment, in the twinkling of an eye, at the last trump: for the trumpet shall sound, and the dead shall be raised incorruptible, and we shall be changed. I Corinthians 15:52

Some lessons are learned the hard way.

A person gave us a small amount of money. He gave no instructions and we foolishly did not ask how he wanted the money spent. We had been very actively communicating with these people by email and thought we knew them. We used the money for something for the two of us. Something we had not had in a long time. We thought the people would be pleased that they had brought some pleasure into the lives of missionaries.

But we could not have been more wrong. When I sent the thank you note complete with details of how much we enjoyed the gift they gave us, they returned a sharp reply. They had intended for the money to be spent in the ministry – not the way we spent it. I immediately took personal funds of the same amount and put in our Bible fund and wrote and told them. But these people were so disappointed that we were "caught up in earthly pleasures" (as they described it) that they broke off all communication. I have not heard from to this day.

Over the years I had managed multi-million dollar projects at the office and never once was I accused of mishandling even one penny of that money. And here I was on the mission field less than a year and had already messed up! If the man had rammed a knife in my stomach and twisted it, it would not have hurt as much. I cried bitterly. I examined my heart. Was I really caught up in earthly pleasures? If I was, I know a place where I could get a whole lot more of 'em than here in Mongolia!

I have moved on but I learned a valuable lesson. Now every

penny we receive goes into the ministry. If anyone wants me to have an earthly pleasure, they are going to have to mail it to me in a box!

The Old Becomes Fresh and New

One of the benefits of going on the foreign mission field is that things appear fresh and new to us. Did someone sneak verses into my Bible? I have been reading God's Word for several decades and never before have I seen so many passages dealing with "teaching the nations", "telling the nations" and "go to all people". Scriptures that had become routine are now alive and vibrant and real to me like never before!

My sister sent me a CD of Twila Paris that included the simple, unchanged melody of "Leaning on the Everlasting Arms". I must have sung and/or played that song thousands of times, but suddenly it became more real than ever before. I challenge you to listen to this old hymn with your heart:

> What a fellowship! What a joy divine!
> (My relationship with my Lord is more intimate than ever before!)
> Leaning on the Everlasting Arms!
> (We could never do what we are doing without a lot of leaning.)
> I have blessed peace with my Lord so dear.
> (There is no greater peace than submitting to God's will for your life.)
> Leaning on the Everlasting Arms!
>
> O how sweet to walk in this pilgrim way.
> (Pilgrim - that's what I feel like in this foreign land.)
> Leaning on the Everlasting Arms!
> O how bright the path grows from day to day.
> (My faith grows with each passing day.)
> Leaning on the Everlasting Arms!
>
> What have I to dread, what have I to fear?

(Not religious law changes. Not language study. Not failure.)
Leaning on the Everlasting Arms!
I have blessed peace with my Lord so near.
(I feel nearer than ever before but I know my Lord has not moved. I must be the one who moved!)
Leaning on the Everlasting Arms!

Leaning, Leaning - safe and secure from all alarms
Leaning, Leaning - leaning on the Everlasting Arms!

Thank you Lord for being there to lean on!

An Honor to Be in This Place

Sometimes I start to feel sorry for myself and get lonely and depressed, but then when I see unsaved Mongolians hearing God's Word, that is all that matters. My piddly complaints and tears are not important in light of the gospel. What an honor to be in this place at this time.

Chapter Eight

HAIR-RAISING ADVENTURES

Hair and personal appearance have never been the most important things in my life, but you do need a decent haircut occasionally.

My Faith Haircut

The Bible says faith is the *substance of things hoped for, the evidence of things not seen. Hebrews 11:1* However, I have a new definition for faith – crawling into a chair to have your hair cut by someone who speaks not one word of English and your Mongolian hair vocabulary includes only the word for "cut". Hal and I had each had a bad haircut so I decided to try and find a new hairdresser. The only good thing about a bad haircut here is that it costs less than a $1.00.

Dema asked if I would like to try her hairdresser. Her hair always looked nice so I agreed. She took me the first time but from then on I went by myself. OK. Now for the word picture of this place:

The building was like all others – concrete block, ugly, old and needing maintenance terribly. After tromping across the trash and broken glass, you go into the building – down into the basement. You have to open a large metal door to go down the stairs. They are dirty (of course), narrow and very small. (My foot hung off.) You have to duck your head to avoid the pipes overhead. At the bottom of the stairs, you make a U-turn. Go past the seamstress shop where people and sewing machines are jammed in like you wouldn't believe. Go to the end of the hall – dodging again the low-hanging pipes that are overhead. Turn left twice and you are at the hairdresser.

The shampoo bowl is a sink - like my kitchen sink. You sit in a straight chair, lean your head back and hold a plastic apron thing around your neck so the water runs into the sink. Very little water pressure. Sometimes the water is warm. Sometimes not. There are no hydraulic lift chairs. Just one height. You either sit up tall or scrunch down as needed. The only natural light is from the one window that is at the ceiling. After they towel dry your hair, they hang the towel over the pipes to dry. (I try not to think about how many times the towel was used before I got there.)

The good thing is the lady is an excellent hair cutter. I am convinced you are either born with that talent or you are not.

Now the price...$3.00! I always tip her well because I can't get used to these prices. Now don't tell anyone because when they hear these prices....and with our beautiful weather (hey we don't just dream of a White Christmas!) everyone will want to come to Mongolia as missionaries! I'm sure they will. There will be no one left at home to hold down the fort!

Getting a Permanent

I got a permanent. Doesn't sound like a big deal, huh? Well, I said that getting my hair cut by a person who speaks not one word of English takes faith. Well that's like mustard seed faith. Getting a permanent here in Mongolia takes watermelon seed faith in my opinion.

Now you may ask, why on earth would you get a perm in Mongolia? Well, my hair is fine and flat with not a natural bend in it. Any curl or poof you have ever seen in my hair was put there artificially. Besides hat hair was driving me nuts. Now in the States you might deal with hat hair after a ball game or after working in the yard. Here you must wear a hat if you go outside for anything in the winter time (which means October – May). When I moved here, I

Hair-Raising Adventures

thought "I'll just buy a cute hat and leave it on all day!" Well, that's not the Mongolian way. You are expected to remove your hat when you go indoors. So hat hair is a daily event here. I opted for a perm.

I took a note from my neighbor to my hairdresser because there is no Mongolian word for perm – only a Russian one which I guess is appropriate since they usually give Russian perms. I racked my brain to try and remember if I ever knew a Russian with a nice perm.

The rods they use are wooden. The irregularity of them makes me think they are individually handcarved. The wood looks like the wood of a clothes pin except in the middle it is darkened from the chemicals. It is shaped like an hourglass with a sling-shot type notch on each end. She wrapped my hair (no end papers – there are very few single-use products in this country) and then used a rubberband in a figure eight through each notch to hold it in place. The rods are longer than those used in the States so more hair was put on each rod.

Then she wrapped a towel around my face while she applied the chemicals. I couldn't see anything (I call that blind faith) but it felt like she was using a paint brush to put the chemical on. It smelled like perms used to smell 20 years ago before they prettied up the smell in America.

With a shower cap on, I was to sit under the dryer for ten minutes. I know I heard the Mongolian word for ten and she held up ten fingers. Well, ten minutes came and went and I was still under the dryer. I became a little concerned (which translates easily without language) and she told me again "ten minutes". I protested and she assured me (in Mongolian) that 20 minutes was OK. There was not a lot I could do but depend on her.

While I was under the dryer I noticed two other ladies getting perms but they were farther along in the process than I was. When they removed the rods from the hair of the first lady, it was total frizz! Her hair looked like she had put her finger in one of these 220 volt Mongolian electrical outlets! I tried to tell myself that it was because she was an older lady and her hair was all gray. (I hoped desperately the chemicals would think my light hair was blond – not gray.)

The second lady had black hair and when they removed the rods from her hair, it was curled – not frizzed. I prayed that I would look more like Lady #2.

It was an exciting day in the beauty shop. The sink fell off the wall. If the girl had not caught it and held it, it would have ripped the drain pipe out of the wall also. They went out in the hall and came back in just a couple minutes with a wooden brace that they rammed under the sink to hold it up. I tried not to put any of my head's weight on it when they rinsed my hair.

They rinsed off the solution and applied neutralizer with a sponge. It was a foamy solution. Then I got to sit again. (Just like in the States – many steps and lots of waiting.) When they took the rods out of my hair, I looked more like Lady #1 than Lady #2.

They gave me a 30 minute head massage and moisturizer treatment – which is heavenly. The hot water here is recycled from the heating plant. Lord only knows what is in it. Sometimes we can even see what's in it. But my skin and scalp itch all the time. So does everyone else's. So a head massage – especially after a Russian perm – sounded like a good thing. Besides I thought it might relieve my stress of wondering how I would look.

After a trim and a blow dry, it was OK. Much frizzier than the nice gentle body perms I am accustomed to, but too late to back out now.

Perm, 30 minute moisturizer massage, haircut and blow dry came to a grand total of……..$4.50. Yep.

A few weeks later I finally made friends with my hair again. It was tighter (read that as frizzier) than I was accustomed to, but hey – when I took my hat off – my hair boinged right back.

Got any mountains you want moved? I have the faith!

Jenny aka Curly

I'm not becoming Gary.

This was written to a friend of ours named Gary.

Hello from Mongolia! Hope you and your family are doing fine.

Hair-Raising Adventures

When you get a letter from the mission field, you expect something really spiritual, huh? Well, this is me writing. I could tell you all kinds of spiritual things because God is taking wonderful care of us! It is so exciting to live on the edge and have God's guiding hand be so obvious every day!

But I'm writing to tell you that I thought of you yesterday and I laughed. Now I doubt if you had access or took the time to read an earlier writing that I did about going to the hairdresser. I know I'm running the risk of losing you here, but you really have to picture the beauty shop where I go to get the full picture of what I am going to tell you. So here is the description.

See description above.

I've been getting really good haircuts here and my neighbor recommended this hairdresser for perms. So I went Friday to get a perm – a true act of faith! After my hair survived the Russian chemicals, they gave me a moisturizer treatment and a full head massage. It was wonderful! I have had them before. I haven't learned the Mongolian word for this treatment (none of the people there speak a word of English) but I just mime a massage and loll my eyes around and they know immediately what I want.

So after they goop your hair and massage it, you sit for about ten minutes. The shop was really quiet yesterday with only one other customer who soon left and all the operators took a break upstairs. So I was sitting there by myself and decided to check out the jar from which they gooped my hair. (I read cereal boxes at the breakfast table too.) One side was in something I couldn't read but the other side was in English – Asian version English. English that is written by Asians has lots of transpositions and often includes words that are almost correct. For example one beauty shop has a sign that says "Beauty Saloon". I'm not sure what beverage they serve you while you get your hair done. You get used to Asian spelling after a while and you can always figure out what they mean.

So the goop was ginseng treatment. It is supposed to moisturize your hair, be good for your scalp, strengthen your hair and .... here it is....PREVENT YOU FROM BECOMING GARY. Now I know in my heart, they meant gray. But your face came to my mind and I sat there in that deserted beauty shop in the basement of a run-down building in Ulaanbaatar and laughed out loud as I jokingly thanked God that I had received a treatment so that I would not become Gary!

When I retold the incident to Hal, I laughed harder than I did the first time and Hal even laughed. (You know what an accomplishment that is!) Hal said I had a strange sense of humor. Well, I had a rough day at school on Friday. Took a horrible test that I know I did very poorly on. Cried as I walked to the trolleybus alone and then went to get my hair done. So maybe I was just overdue for a silly, belly laugh.

Thank you for allowing me to laugh about you. Love, Jenny

June 4, 2000
Major Accomplishment

I went and got my second permanent. This time it is to combat heat and sweat instead of frost and hat hair. Anyway, last time I went, my neighbor had to write me a note telling the hairdresser what I wanted done. I handed it to her and felt just like a child. This time I had learned the words to say in class and I rehearsed them with my neighbor at Wednesday night Bible Study and on Friday I boldly marched into the beauty shop and told my hairdresser what I wanted and she understood me!! How exciting! OK, so it doesn't take much to excite me. But I'll take these milestones any time I can achieve them!

Chapter Nine

TEACHING OLD TONGUES NEW TRICKS

For thou are sent to a people of a strange speech and of a hard language, whose words thou canst not understand. Ezekiel 3:5-6 (OK so I've modified this verse a bit.)

Language learning has been one of the most frustrating, discouraging aspects of our work. We thought we would study one (maybe two) years and then be able to teach and counsel in Mongolian. How foolish of us! It is at least ten times harder than any of us expected. We have been told that most people do not become fluent for about six years. At the time of this writing we have been here three years and are still struggling.

The early days of language learning were particularly difficult. I honestly believe it was more than us just being old and dumb. I believe satan tried (and is trying) to block our language learning. He knows we are learning Mongolian for one reason only – to share the good news of God's love. If he could have stopped us dead in our tracks back in 1999, it would have been a great victory for him.

I'm a pretty down-to-earth person. I don't see visions or hear voices or anything, but I believe I came face to face with a demon on a couple of occasions.

Old and Dumb

One day in late September 1999 I was sitting in language class. I was so frustrated, I couldn't think straight. The teacher was teaching but I couldn't hear a word she said because in my head I was hearing "You're too old and you're too dumb to ever learn this language. Too old and dumb.....old and dumb." Over and over like a roar in my head. Thankfully I recognized that a force of evil was making me think this. I noticed that the pronouns were "you" like someone accusing me instead of "I" like me talking to myself about my inability.

I bowed my head and quietly prayed *"greater is he that is in (me) than he that is in the world. I John 4:4b* Leave me alone!" And immediately the "old and dumb recording" in my head stopped. I could hear the teacher again. My eyes and ears cleared and I continued my lesson. Praise the Lord for the power of His word!

You Can't Do This

In December 1999 one day I left school alone because I had stayed after class to work with my tutor. I had had a particularly frustrating day. It was starting to snow lightly. I bundled up including wrapping the scarf around my head to cover my nose and mouth. As I walked, I heard that same voice in my head. This time it said "You cannot do this!" I began to cry because it sounded so true. But quickly I recognized the accusation of the evil one and outloud – into my scarf – I said "You're right!" Agreeing with the devil? Yes. "You're right. On my own I can't do it, but *I can do all things through Christ which strengtheneth me. Philippians 4:13* That includes speaking Mongolian."

Again the heavy load was lifted. The horrible thoughts stopped. I walked on to the trolleybus singing (out loud into my scarf) – "We are more than conquerors through Him that loved us so. The Christ who died on Calvary is the greatest power we know!"

Will language study ever end?

I'd like to tell you that miraculously I became fluent. I didn't. I have spent countless hours in class and untold hours doing homework and practicing Mongolian. I still struggle and sometimes I get very discouraged. But I know that when I am face to face with the forces of evil, God's Word is sufficient. It's all I need. Have we missed out on awesome things because we have underestimated the power of God's Word? Maybe.

More than once I have wondered why God called us here. Surely there are younger, talented people He could have called to come and do this work. Those bright people could already be fluent and here we are plodding along with translators hoping we live long enough to speak Mongolian. Maybe God has called those people and they have not yet answered the call. Or maybe we are the right people for this task although it doesn't seem to be so – in human thinking. Once again I was reminded that God does not want our ability. He wants our availability.

Moses and Aaron

One day as I pondered this language dilemma, I ran across the story of Moses and Aaron. Oh how I identified with Moses when he said:

> *O my Lord, I am not eloquent...but I am slow of speech, and of a slow tongue. Exodus 4:10*

Yes, God knew that Moses was linguistically challenged (*Exodus 4:11*) and He knew that Aaron could speak well (*Exodus 4:14*). God did not call Aaron to lead the Children of Israel and there was probably a reason for that.

Aaron was the one who after Moses was absent just a short time (*Exodus 32:1*) had the people bring their gold and he melted it and formed a golden calf for the people to worship. (*Exodus 32:2-4*) Moses challenged Aaron asking what on earth the people did to him to make him do that. (*Exodus 32:21*) Moses obviously had a lot of confidence in Aaron and couldn't believe he did this on his own. Aaron replied that they put the gold in the fire and out popped the golden calf. (*Exodus 32:24*) Yea right!! Like who would believe that story! Can you imagine what would have happened if Aaron had been in charge the whole time!!

There's a study of two brothers. Aaron tried to hide behind the people. (*Exodus 32:22*) Moses stood between God and the people. (*Exodus 32:31-32*). He even offered himself to bear their sin.

So God knew that fluency was not the most important characteristic. Moses had his faults. He tried to help God free his people by killing one of the Egyptians, (*Exodus 2:12*) but of course that didn't work. Moses just ended up in a 40-year management training program on the backside of the desert! He had a temper problem – breaking the tablets of stone on which God had written the Ten Commandments. (*Exodus 32:19*) The people drove him to distraction out in the wilderness and he had that little incident with the rock *(Numbers 20:8-11)* that cost him dearly *(Numbers 20:12)*.

But Moses had a very close relationship with God. I had never noticed before that when God was really angry with Israel, Moses challenged Him to repent. Repent!!! (*Exodus 32:12*) Can you believe it?!? Now that is being pretty tight with The Almighty! And God did repent! (*Exodus 32:14*) So I guess Moses had no fluency problem when it came to talking to God!

Still thankful to be studying Mongolian. Thankful that fluency is not a prerequisite to serving! Very thankful I continue to find nuggets in God's Word!

March 28, 2000
The Tongue is a Little Member
(And Doesn't Speak Mongolian Very Easily)

In class I was the dumbest one. Everyone else got the answers; I could not come up with a correct response. The teacher patiently worked individually with me as the rest of the class waited. So in case they hadn't notice which student was the slow one, I was clearly identified. I made it through that session with God's help.

To the Tune of "There Will Be Peace in the Valley for Me"

Music is always part of my life – even if I have to rewrite old songs.

> I'm so tired and so weary, but I must go along.
> Till the Mongolian words are in my brain.
> From the dawn's early light to the wee hours of midnight
> I will study this language to gain.
>
> Yes, there will be dative* words coming from me, someday.
> Yes, there will be pronouns in every case upon my tongue, oh Lord I pray.
> There'll be no stuttering, no stammering, no blank looks you'll see.
> There will be Mongolian language from me.

* Mongolian has many cases that English does not have. Dative is just one of them that gives us fits!

Language Snafu
I said "Grandfather".

One night after church we went to Egi and Naara's to celebrate Tsaamba's birthday. Several relatives were there who only speak Mongolian. At one point the twins were climbing all over Hal and Dennis and playing. I used my best Mongolian and pointed to Hal and said (I thought) "one grandfather" and then pointed to Dennis and said (I thought) "two grandfathers". All the Mongolians laughed really hard. I didn't think what I said was that funny. After waiting several minutes for Egi to regain control, he told me that I had said Hal and Dennis were each (as Egi politely put it).....a bosom!!!! OK, back to the books!

You need a small face.

Hal bought a little model ger. It was no small task putting it together so he invited Biaraa and Bilgoon to come over and help put it together. Bilgoon was struggling with a teeny, tiny string. In my very best Mongolian I wanted to say "You need small fingers." Instead I said "You need a small face." OK, so body parts is not my strength in vocabulary! Bilgoon dissolved into laughter and for several minutes could not even tell me what I had said! I simply do not know what these people did for entertainment before we arrived! Still glad to be here on this exciting journey despite the embarrassing moments!

The whole country is handicapped!

Isn't it a shame that everyone in Mongolia has a speech impediment? I don't understand a thing they say. And on top of that, everyone in Mongolia has a hearing problem. They don't understand what I am saying in Mongolian! This observation was from my language classmate Jonathan.

Monglish

When we speak, you never know if English or Mongolian is going to come out. We use Mongolian until we get stumped by a word, throw in the English word and return to Mongolian. We speak Monglish – a new language!

Two Tomorrows

In October 1999 we went to a store on a Tuesday to buy an appliance. We needed to get the money and return on Thursday to get the item. Hal asked me how to say "Thursday" in Mongolian. At that time the days of the week were sorta like learning the books of the Bible. I had to take a running start at it. So as I was thinking in my head (Monday is Nigdeh, Tuesday is Hoyeldeh, Wednesday is….), Hal thought of a way to communicate. He told the man we would return in "hoyel malgosh". That means "two tomorrows". The man understood. We walked out of the store laughing. Whoever heard of two tomorrows – but it worked!

Now we not only know the name for Thursday (and all the other days of the week) without taking a running start, but we can even say "day after tomorrow". But "hoyel malgosh" remains a part of our vocabulary and always will.

April 2, 2000
I spoke no English!

I had a very difficult week for reasons I don't fully understand. I just seemed to be under attack. I didn't come here based on emotions and I certainly am not staying based on emotions. We are staying because we believe this is where God wants us right now.

The high point of my week was on Saturday when I took some shoes to be repaired. I told them what I wanted done. We discussed price and when they would be ready. Then the man asked me if I was German!!! Isn't that great? Do you know what that means? It means I used all Mongolian - so much that he could not tell my nationality. OK, so that may be a silly thing to get excited about but I grab at every little bit of encouragement that I can!

Mongolian Tongue

While enjoying a special dinner one day, Hal asked his Mongolian teacher if he ate Mongolian cow tongue (which was being served), would he become fluent in Mongolian. She immediately answered "Yes. You will moooo just like a Mongolian cow!" OK, back to the books.

Is my face red!!!

I needed to meet with Biaraa and Dema in order to interview Biaraa for a profile I was doing. I was doing really good, clipping along in Mongolian discussing a time we were all available. I meant to say "Let's meet together" but instead I said "Let's sleep together!"

Yes, "meet" and "sleep" start with the same letters, but I do know the difference. How did they get mixed up in my brain? I knew immediately from the look on their faces that I had misspoken. Oh how embarrassing!!! Back to the drawing board! About the time I get a thimbleful of confidence in Mongolian, I fall flat on my face!

Vowel Sounds

One day right after we arrived, Charlotte and I went to the market by ourselves after class because the guys had an appointment at the bank. We were very proud that we handled this on our own – even asking prices in Mongolian and most of the time understanding the prices they quoted us. We handled the money and carried everything in a bag. We agreed to meet the guys outside the State Store. They weren't there when we arrived so we decided to sit down and have a soft drink. As I eased my body into the chair, I moaned....oh, ahh, ooo, errr, uuuuug. I asked Charlotte which Mongolian vowels sounds I had missed!

Language Study

It would be so wonderful if when a person made a commitment to a particular foreign mission field, if God would insert that foreign language into the missionary's head, but it does not work that way. Language study is the first huge challenge a foreign missionary faces. Here is a little about the challenge of learning the Mongolian language.

Maybe you are wondering why it is so difficult (other than the fact we are retraining 50+ year-old tongues). Maybe you think you just learn new words to replace English words. Not so!

Alphabet: First you learn a new alphabet. Mongolian has some letters that are the same as English letters and some that look like English letters but have completely different sounds so that involves "unlearning and relearning". Example: B sounds like V or W; H sounds like N; X sounds like H; a backwards N sounds like E or I, P sounds like L - trilled; plus there are totally new sounds to learn – some of which seem similar to rearranging congestion from a post nasal drip.

Words: There are many words for "have" depending on whether (1) the item is present and specific or (2) something you have to check on to determine if you have it or (3) if the thing is always or nearly always there. Confusing? Definitely.

Sentence Structure: The verb is always at the end of the sentence. ("I like you" becomes "I you like".) Mongolian has <u>post</u>-positions (store to) instead of <u>pre</u>positions (to the store). Mongolian is an agglutinative language which means it has stem words with suffixes added to make grammatical changes. A word can have many suffixes – each one changing the meaning of the word slightly. So sentences like: "John went with his father to the countryside. They will ride horses every day." becomes (in Mongolian) "John fatherwithhis countryside to went. They day every horses ride will."

Direct Objects: If the object of a sentence is specific (not general), it requires a different suffix. If you are like us, we had not discussed parts of speech since high school. We speak English without much thought - which sometimes shows! Now we must think about the components of a sentence in order to speak it correctly in Mongolian.

We long to share the gospel with Mongolians in their native tongue. We pray *that God would open unto us a door of utterance, to speak the mystery of Christ. Colossians 4:3.*

Definitions

Communication is more than just forming words. It is speaking concepts. Here are some Mongolian definitions we learned from experience:

Not far:	Anything up to five miles (walking) and 100 miles (driving).
Not long:	15 – 30 minutes or more.
Not late:	15 minutes after the appointed hour is "on time".
Not cold:	Anything warmer than tens degrees below zero.
Not hard:	The latest Mongolian grammar lesson (not hard if you are Mongolian).

The last one: Until the next one. Example: That is the last pot hole in the road - until the next one.

Stubborn is a good thing.

I think I figured out why we were sent here. We are stubborn! Only the most stubborn person would stay at language study that is this hard! You never knew stubbornness was a positive attribute, huh?

The train left the depot!

The first week of my second year at school was particularly hard for me. Dennis and Charlotte settled in as a class of two. Hal was rotating through multiple teachers – which he likes. All my classmates from last year had left the school. So they put me with a different class that was technically at the same level as I was; however, their speaking was far better and faster than mine. (Living a month in the countryside this past summer didn't hurt their Mongolian any!) The prior year when I changed classes, I was behind everyone else. I felt like I was chasing a train that was leaving the station. But I managed to catch up and jump on the caboose and stayed with that "train" the rest of the year.

However, in this class the train had already pulled out of the station and picked up speed and I was left standing on the platform. There was no chance of catching up. Mongolian teachers always teach to the smartest student in the class – which has never been me so I'm accustomed to that observer role, but this was ridiculous. I estimate I was grasping maybe 25% of what was being said! Not enough to give me any confidence that what I heard was what was actually said. Sometimes I did not even have a frame of reference as a basis for guessing. I didn't know if we were discussing a horse or a tea party!

So I asked to be changed. They arranged for me to have private teachers – four days a week. I had absorbed more of the grammar from my earlier class than I or the teacher expected, but the overwhelmed feeling was preventing me from doing the speaking I needed to do. Intimidation doesn't do much for my confidence!

October 8, 2000
First Time I Shared the Gospel in Mongolian

Well, I experienced another first this week. On Friday my teacher said we were just going to have conversation (in Mongolian of course) for the entire session. She proceeded to tell me a story about reincarnation. At the end she told me that some Mongolians believe if you do good things, you go to heaven. If you don't do enough good things, then you must return to try again.

She finished and then I had to retell the story to her – so she could be sure I understood what she said. I did fairly well through most of it – getting all the basic facts accurate. I got a little mixed up at the end – probably because I was having to spit out reincarnation stuff. When I finished, she said "Do Americans believe in reincarnation?" Well, open the door and ask me to come in!

So I proceeded to give her the plan of salvation – in Mongolian of course. It was so rough. I definitely need some work on basic terms. She had heard the gospel before so she understood what I was saying, but she is not saved. She is very confused between Buddhism and Christianity. Also, the person who shared the gospel with her made her feel that Mongolians (and only Mongolians) are bad. Fortunately, I had all the words to tell her that everyone is a sinner – Mongolians, Americans, Europeans – none of us can do enough good things to stand before God but with Jesus' blood applied to our hearts, we appear clean before our God.

So please pray for all the teachers we come in contact with. We are walking Bibles to them. Only now – in our second year of school – do we have enough language to start to share the gospel and each of us has opportunity – without forcing ourselves on them – which is not the style of our team. Pray for us that we will continue to gather the language skills we need to share Christ to a lost and searching people.

Random Thought

God made a donkey speak. He opened Sarah's womb when she was old. Surely He can make these old tongues speak!

Plunging Ahead

On Friday I had Bible Reading in class – a regular occurrence now. Then the teacher had questions prepared about the passage we read. She believes if you do good things, you become a Christian and go to heaven. No faith involved – only works. In the past I have tried to explain to her that we cannot work our way to heaven.

Anyway, on Friday the subject was again on this topic. At first I noticed that she was unhappy as I spoke. I thought my grammar was wrong. I stopped and asked her if it was OK. She distractedly said "Sentence Correct" but maintained the troubled look on her face. She seemed so interested that I decided to just go for it. If she wanted to stop to correct my grammar – fine. If not, I was going to plunge ahead.

And so I did. For 30 minutes I got to speak on the plan of salvation and how we cannot possibly do enough good things to earn heaven. I'm quite certain she understood what I was saying because of the look of concern on her face.

Pray that I continue to have opportunities to share Christ with her. And please keep praying that the Mongolian will kick in one of these days – for our entire team. At this particular session, I was far more articulate than normal. I am quite certain God was helping me. I need that all the time!

February 25, 2001
A Baby Prayer

This week I did something for the first time. I prayed in Mongolian. Just a few sentences. Baby sentences really. But it was a wonderful experience. When I went to visit a friend at the hospital, I decided it was time I was able to pray a simple prayer in Mongolian. It's the perfect place to use my Mongolian. God always understands what I am praying and most people will not laugh at you while you are praying! This was a milestone for me. Well....a mile pebble.

I'm not learning Mongolian to joke with the locals, but it sure is fun!

At a church fellowship I saw a man eating buuz (meat dumplings) and chocolates - together. Yuk!! In my best Mongolian, I asked him if he was pregnant. I know he understood because for a few minutes he was laughing too hard to eat.

Like a Child

One Sunday morning before anyone else arrived at church, Dennis and I did a role play. He acted like a child student - asking me questions about Jesus. I answered them. His questions and my answers were all in Mongolian. We went for probably ten sentences or more! What fun! It sounds so silly now that I have written it down, but I guess you have to go through the 18 months of struggle that we have been through to understand the simple joys of communicating the gospel in your second language.

Thank you Lord for precious fun memories.

Oh For a Thousand Tongues

> Definition: Tongue (1) the soft, moveable organ in the mouth; (2) the ability to speak; (3) a language.

We went to the closing ceremony for the school year. One of the students from America had been taking lessons to learn to play the horsehead fiddle – the official musical instrument of Mongolia. He did a lovely job of playing a traditional Mongolian melody. Then he played a most appropriate hymn and stood and sang it acapelo:

> Oh for a thousand tongues to sing my great Redeemer's praise.

The glories of my God and King, the triumph of His grace.
Jesus the name that calms our fears. That bids our sorrows cease.
'Tis music in the sinner's ear. 'Tis life and health and peace.

How many times during my 50+ years of life have I sung that hymn on a Sunday morning – mindlessly, without it touching my heart? But that Thursday morning in early July at a graduation ceremony, I appreciated the words of that hymn for the first time. Tears ran down my cheeks unchecked! Within the four walls of that school I had spent hundreds of hours struggling with dative, genitive, ablative and accusative cases and trying to form sounds that refused to roll off my tongue.

Once again as I have so many, many times before, I asked God to give me not a thousand tongues. Just one more – Mongolian. So I can share the name that calms our fears…that bids our sorrows cease.

That utterance may be given unto me, that I may open my mouth boldly, to make known the mystery of the gospel. Ephesians 6:19

Mongolians live in white tents called gers because they are a nomadic people.

Hai and Jenny

A ger on the outskirts of Ulaanbaatar.

Mongolia is said to be the last horse culture in the world.

One-third of the population of Mongolia lives in Ulaanbaatar, the capital and largest city.

In the countryside animals still provide the main mode of transportation.

Winter is the longest season which is marked by extremely low temperatures.

Ulaanbaatar is a city of extreme contrasts.

Children in the countryside.

Chapter Ten

CHRISTMAS IS NOT FOR WIMPS

November 5, 2000

"It's beginning to look a lot like Christmas. Everywhere I go." (Wait a minute! It's three weeks until Thanksgiving!)

"I'm dreaming of a White Christmas!" (You ain't dreaming honey!)

"Sleighbells ring, are you listenin'? In the lane snow is glistening. It's a beautiful sight. We're happy tonight – walking in a winter wonderland!"

Yep, winter has finally arrived in Mongolia. It has been snowing all day and even Ulaanbaatar is beautiful – like a matronly old woman with a new dress on. I really think winter might be my favorite season here. OK, someone is sure to remind me of that along next March when I am so sick of snow I could scream!

Christmas letters are written in November or early December, while Christmas is still just a beautiful plan. Thus the great attitude. Here are excerpts.

Christmas Letter 1999
Ulaanbaatar, Mongolia

Hello to Family and Friends:

I trust God has blessed you abundantly this past year and you are rejoicing in a wonderful holiday season! No matter what has happened to us, we can rejoice because no matter how terrible the circumstances may seem, God has approved everything that comes our way and He wants only the best for His children. Long ago when Mary faced the scorn of society because she was bearing a child out of wedlock, she could easily have wondered how anything good could come of those circumstances. But it was all ordered by God and what a wondrous event it was!

God has enriched our lives so much this past year that I could not possibly capture it on paper! A highpoint of the year was May 29 when Christopher and Stephanie were married. A glorious wedding day when another God-honoring home was established. We now have a wonderful daughter-in-love (that's no typo). Our children are serving the Lord which brings us great joy. *I have no greater joy than to hear that my children walk in truth. III John 4.*

We have not officially launched a work here but we have many opportunities to minister to the people. They are so hungry to be taught God's Word. It is really thrilling. They have only had the gospel here since 1990 so there are many young Christians who need to be taught. We are so thankful God has chosen us to be a part of this ministry!

Our life has changed dramatically! Living in a developing country is quite an experience. Living for over 70 years under communism affects the way people think. The most amazing part of the whole year is how we immediately felt at home here even though everything around us is strange!

So I have always wondered what Christmas would be like without all the commercialism. No gaudy holiday displays before Thanksgiving, no 40,000 verses of "The 12 Days of Christmas", no Salvation Army bell ringing, no TV commercials repeated over and over, no Santa Claus stealing the show, no crowds at the mall, no holiday stress. Well, we are about to find out! Mongolia does not celebrate Christmas because it is primarily a Buddhist country. The Christians celebrate privately in their homes. One thing for sure – we'll have a white Christmas. We have had snow since mid-October and since the temperature has not been above 25 degrees F in two months, it sticks.

Our children are going to Mom and Dad's for Christmas. It will be a difficult time for the boys and Hal and me, but last July as we said goodbye God gave us all the peace that passes all understanding. It was truly amazing! He continues to give the children and us the strength to be apart and we believe Christmas will be a time of peace on earth and more importantly peace in our hearts.

As you gather with your friends and family, I ask that you say a prayer not only for our family but also for all the missionaries around the world who are separated from loved ones during the holiday season. Did I do that the past 50 years when I was in the States? No. But I certainly will for every Christmas season remaining in my life and now that I have made you aware, I ask that you remember missionaries also.

We are grateful for all the people back home who support us financially, spiritually and emotionally. We couldn't take this exciting journey without the love and support of all of you. Christmas on the mission field is not for wimps!

Love, Hal and Jenny

The school party was fun. So what's so hard about Christmas on the foreign field?

December 19, 1999
Christmas Party

God is really good to us. I guess I've said that before. We knew this was going to be a little different Christmas. Well that's an understatement, is it not? But I think God is going to bless us more than we ever expected.

To the Ends of the Earth!

Last Wednesday after our Big Test, the school planned a Christmas Party. They divided us up by nationality. We didn't really have much choice in participating. So we went along with their plan. They wanted a table centerpiece, our flag, name tags, food from our country, a greeting (in Mongolian), a song and a game. So we got everything ready – out of obligation. Well, despite our reluctant attitude in the beginning, it turned out to be one of the best holiday parties I have ever attended!

The food was fantastic. There were tables representing Hong Kong, Korea, Taipei, Finland, America (three tables) and of course, Mongolia. There were probably 100 people there. Everyone joined right in. We have found that Mongolian people are like children when it comes to games and parties. Nothing is too juvenile for them and they have so much fun, everyone around them has fun. Of course, people who leave home and go to a place like Mongolia – usually are pretty hang loose also.

I had re-written the 12 Days of Christmas to be appropriate for language school. I spent a whole 20 minutes on it. After our team sang it, everyone raved like it was something really special! Go figure. I spend a lot more time on my Mongolian and no one is impressed! Dennis presented John 3:16 in Mongolian and a few words about why we celebrate Christmas.

The group from Hong Kong did a drama of Mary and Joseph – in Mongolian – and we understood them! A first - the Christmas story in Mongolian. It was a hoot! We loved it! We heard Silent Night in four different languages, sung by native speakers. How special!

The Mongolian teachers (none of whom are Christians) heard the gospel in every single presentation. Someone commented that there was more Christ in Christmas here than in the States. I believe it. Here there is no reason to celebrate unless you are worshipping Christ.

So we came home very much in the mood for the holidays. What a blessing! A Christmas memory I will never forget!

And here is the prettied up writing that I sent that week. All of this is true but certain ugly facts were omitted. Don't want to upset the folks back in the States.

December 26, 1999
Christmas

We had many blessings this holiday season. Last Wednesday night after Bible Study we had a wonderful fellowship time with cookies and tea. The Mongolians loved the homemade American cookies.

Then Christmas Day Charlotte and I fixed dinner for 12 of us. Everything turned out really well. All of our staging and planning worked out. Our two oven pans were put to good use and food passed through my tiny oven on cue! The kitchen deck became a walk-in refrigerator/freezer. We put two tables together and our living room became our dining room. The laughter and excitement of Egi and Naara's children bring a lot of comfort and love into our lives.

The really huge blessing I had was to present the Christmas story to the children with flannelgraph - in Mongolian! I worked on it for weeks. I enlisted special prayer partners in the States. With much prayer and practice and God's help, I did it! Our neighbors next door came over. The husband is not saved and he seemed very interested. I was so pleased that he came. It was thrilling to be able to minister in Mongolian - even though it was in children's language. The closing of my story was "Jesus came to earth because He loves you. He loves me. He loves all people." That part just rolled off my tongue. I could say it with feeling. I long for the day that all my Mongolian will roll easily off the tongue!

And here is the rest of the story about Christmas on the foreign field.

Christmas Memories – 1999
Christmas on the foreign field is not for wimps!

I made an important discovery. Although homesickness feels

like a terminal illness, you will not die from it! With God's grace, I got through the holiday season without my children.

I thought being away from my kids at Thanksgiving was hard. For some reason, my birthday was a difficult day also. But hey, those were a walk in the park compared to being away from my kids on Christmas Day! I cried uncontrollably from the time I got up until noon when I was scheduled to call the children. Like the mother who miraculously has the strength to lift an automobile to rescue her child, I dried it up minutes before the call. I did better after I talked to them, but I really wouldn't wish that pain on my worst enemy!

I had known intellectually for over 20 years that the time would come when I would be away from them on Christmas Day. I just didn't expect it to be both of them the same Christmas and that I wouldn't see them for five months before or for a year afterward!

God has given us wonderful friends here in Mongolia, but the main desire I had was to simply survive the holidays. If I could have gone to sleep on December 22 and woke up on December 26 – that would have been far easier than living through those days.

I was anxious to get back to normal days. I had five months' of practice dealing with the pain of normal days. I didn't have much practice dealing with the pain of holidays.

My prayer that Christmas evening: "Thank you God for the grace to get through this day. I couldn't have done it without You! Please let me fall asleep quickly. I need relief from this pain."

Just Another Day
(Written December 25, 1999)

I looked out over the snowy Mongolian landscape Christmas morning. People were going about their business just like any other day. Going to market. Going to school. A cart went by with a load of sheep carcasses. Another man was peddling fur pelts. A welder was busily working on the construction site. Just another day. No thought of Jesus – whose birth we are celebrating. How sad!

But then I thought – in America people are going about the Christmas business just like any other Christmas. Giving gifts, receiving gifts, shopping till they drop, uncorking champagne, singing about Rudolph and snowmen and going to parties. Just another Christmas. No thought of Jesus – whose birth we are celebrating. How sad!

Long ago in Bethlehem people were going about their business just like any other day. Buying, selling, paying taxes, filling hotels to overflowing. Except for the shepherds, there was no notice of the most important birth ever to occur. Just another day. No thought of Jesus – whose birth was occurring. How sad!

Jesus' first coming gained very little attention among mankind. The celebration of that day is losing attention with each passing year. But one day soon, He will return for a second time and the whole world will acknowledge His arrival. Every knee will bow. It will not be just another day. How glorious it will be!

For the Lord himself shall descend from heaven with a shout, with the voice of the archangel, and with the trump of God.
I Thessalonians 4:16

And the second Christmas rolled around on cue. More glowing excerpts from my holiday letter.

Christmas Letter 2000

Dear Precious Friends and Family:

As I reread the Christmas story for the umphundredth time, again I found something fresh and new (to me anyway). God's Word continually amazes me! Herod pretended to want to worship Christ but it was all a sham. How many people make a show of celebrating Christmas but have no real desire to know the Christ whose birth we celebrate? Every day of the year, may we worship Him in spirit and in truth.

We have had a very exciting Year 2000 here in Mongolia. God has given us so many chances to share His love with the Mongolian people. We are in our second year of language study. It only gets more difficult with the growing complexity of grammar, but we remain committed to ministering to these precious souls in their mother tongue. God continues to bless us with good health, a deep satisfaction that we are where He wants us right now and an unexplainable excitement caused by the opportunities we see here in this faraway land.

We had three groups of guests this past year. In April Lynn and Brenda, our mission trainers from Florida, came as our first guests. Then our dear friend, Anne and her sister-in-law, Verla, came in time for Naadam in July. Naadam is the big sports event of the year here. It involves archery, wrestling and horse racing. Then Bill and Rosie from our sponsoring church and Harold from Florida came in late August. We tried to show all of our guests a good time so maybe they would be willing to venture back to see us again.

After our mission team met for worship in our livingroom for several months, in April we rented a large apartment for our church services - near where we live. Nine of us worshipped that first Sunday. Now we often have 20+ on Sundays and 12 or more at Wednesday night Bible Study. God has blessed beyond our wildest imaginations! We have seen souls saved – including our next door neighbors - and we have had several baptized. The greatest thrill is to present the gospel to people who have never before heard the tidings of great joy. The wonderful good news that has become old to some of us is received with wide-eyed amazement by those who are hearing for the first time how much God loves them! What a joy to be the messenger!

Last year I asked all my family and friends to start a tradition of praying for missionary families on Christmas Day. It is a very difficult time of year to be away from loved ones. Please keep that tradition alive this year by praying for all of us who have ...*forsaken houses, brethren, sisters, father, mother, children, and lands for Christ's sake... Matthew   19:29.* On behalf of missionaries around the world – thank you!

We pray you have a wonderful Christmas.
Love, Hal and Jenny

December 3, 2000
Less is More

Christmas has arrived in our apartment. I put out all the decorations. In the States it took me several days to decorate the tree and set out all the ornaments and things. Here it took me about one hour and I diddled around. But the things I have here are appreciated far more than the overabundance that I had in the States. My Mongolian collection is starting to grow though. This year we have the tree that was sent to us by the ladies in Martinez. A small artificial tree decorated with dozens of little cards – each signed by a family at our sponsoring church. It is our "love-ly" tree.

Naara and I are working on the Christmas program at church. For years I have worked on such programs. I remember trying to think of something different....interesting.....a unique angle...... exciting...even cute. But the last few years before coming here, I had returned to God's Word – plain and simple in all of its power and beauty. You can't beat it. And that is what we are going to present here. Naara and I are very excited. Can't wait. It's just like decorations – less is more. More appreciated. More beautiful. We hope to have a packed house (which won't take too many more than our regulars).

December 24, 2000

Our week was filled with preparations for our special services today. And special they were! 43 people came to church! That's our highest number so far. We can comfortably seat 30 so we were really scrunched - kids sat on laps, Charlotte and I sat in an adjoining room and Bilgoon sat in the hallway. Dennis and the translator never sat.

For the program portion, we used the large nativity scene that was sent to us by a lady at the Martinez church. It is pretty incredible even for American eyes but the Mongolians really loved it! Everyone (except elderly and disabled people) stood during the program.

We had enough food for everyone. A mix of American sandwiches and Mongolian buuz, horshol (fried pies with meat inside) and fish. The people returned to their chairs and ate off their laps. Cozy, close fellowship, but they loved it! Many have promised to return. We pray that they do!

Some were hearing the Christmas story for the first time. What a special time! My former boss put into words why it is so special for us. In an email this week she said "Jenny, it must be particularly poignant to celebrate the birth of Christ with those who first learned of His story from you!"

Hope everyone has a wonderful, peaceful Christmas! Jenny

Manna

As I packed away Christmas things, I enjoyed the red and green fabric one more time. I look forward to seeing my children this coming year but I thought ahead to next Christmas – when we will be back here in Mongolia. A third Christmas without my children! The pain already pierces my gut at the very thought. How will I possibly endure that? God helped me through that first difficult Christmas away from home, and He helped us through this past Christmas. But a third one? Only God knows how many Christmases will pass before we will again be with our children!

Then God brought to my mind a story from the Old Testament. My active imagination helps me fill in blanks in the Bible. Maybe it happened this way....

Sarah: Elizabeth, please gather another omer of manna for us.

Elizabeth: But Sarah, we have enough manna for today.

Sarah: Yes, but I would like a little extra for tomorrow. Even though we had manna yesterday and the day before, I'd like to be prepared.

Elizabeth: But Moses said take only one day's supply. I fear he will get angry.

Sarah: Think about it! Manna is provided by God. It is a

good thing. Gather it now while we have it!

Elizabeth: OK. But I don't think this is going to work.

Editor's Note: It didn't. The manna rotted. Moses got angry. It was a test. *(Exodus 16).*

OK, Lord. I accept the promise in Philippians 4:19. You have provided all that we have needed to get us through difficult days in the past and I believe you will provide exactly what we need tomorrow....and next Christmas...and the one after that...and the one after that...
And the third Christmas was slightly easier.

December 23, 2001

I've been thinking. That's always dangerous. Cultural traditions and religious traditions get smooshed together, making it difficult to separate the two. We see Mongolians struggle with this - trying to determine which of their customs are Buddhist and which are simply Mongolian. Sometimes they want to throw out everything Mongolian and try to be like Westerners. We didn't come here for that! We came to present Christ whom they can worship as Mongolians.

We have to separate Christianity from Western tradition - and those two are smooshed also. This week I did some real profound teaching when I told a Mongolian friend that Jingle Bells is not a church song. She was quite surprised. But it's not. They think anything from America is Christian. Wish that it were so but it's not.

Home for the holidays is such a good idea - so cozy and warm. Songs have been written about it. Most holiday movies deal with going home for Christmas. Surely it is scriptural...or at least religious.....or is it?

Mary wasn't at home that first Christmas morning. She had traveled to the hometown of her almost husband - to pay taxes. What a nuisance! And of course, now was the time she was ready to deliver. Wouldn't you know it? Her mother wasn't there to help, nor her aunts, nor her cousin Elizabeth. She had no labor coach. Mary must have been a little frightened. She knew her pregnancy was supernatural, but how would the birth be? Would it be normal? Not that she knew what a normal birth felt like. Maybe she would die giving birth. The angel didn't say anything about after the baby was born. Maybe God only needed her body to produce His son and He might not need her afterwards.

Joseph was a kind, loving man. He had not made a public spectacle of her - like he had every right to do. But did he know anything about birthing babies? And they had ended up in a barn - not exactly a woman's idea of a proper nursery for her baby.

She was not at home that first Christmas and probably not for several after that - as they had to go to Egypt to protect Jesus from King Herod's jealous wrath. That must have been hard - to be in a strange land, away from family, with a strange language and foreign customs.

No, if those first Christmas Days are an example to us, then home has no part of the holiday. Father, forgive my whining at this time of year. Help me remember that we are here to tell these precious people about the most wonderful gift of all times - God's son!

Merry Christmas from the ends of the earth! Jenny

December 30, 2001

How wonderful is our God! I trust all of you had a blessed Christmas. Thank you to all who prayed for us during this season. I know we could never do this (any day of the year) without the many, many prayer warriors who are taking our names to the throne of God - pleading on our behalf.

I figured the way to deal with feeling blue was to do something for someone else. So on Christmas Eve I put together a block party - Mongolian style - inviting the neighbors on our floor. I baked cookies and made fudge. I gave some to our food vendor whose husband is in the hospital and some to the guard's family in our building. The rest of the goodies went on a tray - served with tea. After some polite talk, the conversation turned to questions about the Bible. Hal ended up teaching a one-hour Bible lesson. What a joy! Thank you Lord!

Christmas Day we went to dinner with Dennis and Charlotte. The guys ate gazelle. Charlotte and I stuck with steak. It was good. Then we went to Egi and Naara's for milk tea.

If you want to maintain your clean, uplifting, storybook view of missionaries, then you need to read monthly mission reports. Those are always devoid of any negative or ugly things and you always get a snippet of scripture - appropriate to the theme. What a deal! But my weekly writings ain't a monthly report. You never really get the whole story of missionaries because it is simply too much for foreigners (that would be you folks) to handle. But I try to give you a little glimpse of real life on the foreign field.

So Christmas sounds pretty on paper and parts of it were indeed joyous. And of course I put on a happy face for Dennis and Charlotte. They have their own burdens to carry without dealing with an hysterical helper. And of course the Mongolians only see a joyous Christian in me. But behind the mask - inside the facade - is raw, ugly pain.

The historical view of this situation is "You made it through other Christmases alone. This has got to get easier!" The spiritual view of this situation is "God is with me. What is my problem?" The logical view of this says "You just saw your children. You have talked to your parents and children on the phone. What more do you want?" But the historical view and logical reasoning don't know diddly about pain. And I guess I'm just not as spiritual as I should be because I hurt!

God never said He would remove our dark hours. Only that He would be with us through those dark valleys. And He was! In my darkest hour, I know God is right there - never leaving me for a single second. In fact He feels closer during those times.

So I survived another Christmas. Saturday it dawned on me that although survival is seldom a pretty thing, it is a victorious time. As I did laundry, I had music playing. I love singing in Mongolian and we sing a lot of praise and worship songs from America. But I really miss the old basic hymns. The ones I have sung all my life. The ones where I have all the words memorized. The ones our team sang without accompaniment each Sunday when we first arrived.

But those days are over. Now we sing in Mongolian. But I miss those songs.

Well, I borrowed a CD from Egi and it was 25 Old-Fashioned Songs of Praise. Oh what a time of worship I had that morning! I decided the laundry could wait. I sat in my living room enjoying my old favorites.

I'll Fly Away - What a wonderful thing to look forward to! If your foot can sit still through that song, then you are paralyzed (physically or spiritually).

Leaning on the Everlasting Arms - Hey! That's just what I've been doing this past week. ...What a blessedness, what a peace is mine - leaning on the everlasting arms. Safe and secure.....

Blessed Assurance Jesus is Mine. Oh what a foretaste of glory divine. Heir of salvation, purchase of God. Born of His spirit, washed in His blood. This is my story. This is my song. Praising my Savior all the day long. This is my story. This is my song. Praising my Savior all the day long.

Rob and Ellen told me of one place they worshipped (I don't remember where) that when they reached the chorus of this song, they held up their Bible (this is my story) and in the other hand held up a hymnal (this is my song) during this song. Well, I usually control myself but the last Sunday before we left to come to Mongolia in 1999, the Praise Team at Martinez sang that song and I guess I forgot to control myself. God had moved so mightily on our behalf to get us on our way to Mongolia. I was overcome with thankfulness. So during the chorus I raised my Bible and hymnal. When we went back for furlough this past spring, my sweet Stephanie told me that every time she hears Blessed Assurance, she thinks of me and my Bible and hymnal - and she cries.

Well, Saturday I sat in my living room, singing this hymn, remembering that day in 1999, praising our Lord (and crying of course) and thanking Him for that assurance and also for our precious daughter-in-love.

His Name is Wonderful. He's the great shepherd, the rock of all ages, Almighty God is He. Bow down before Him. Love and adore Him. His Name is Wonderful, Jesus my Lord...I think I can translate that song into Mongolian! Add that to my To Do List.

Sing Oh Sing of My Redeemer. With His blood He purchased me! On the cross He sealed my pardon, paid the debt and made me free!

Great is Thy Faithfulness - Wow! How true! I've lived that song this past week. ....Great is thy faithfulness! Great is thy faithfulness! Morning by morning new mercies I see. All I have needed thy hand has provided. Great is thy faithfulness, Lord unto me!!!

We have heard the joyful sound. Jesus Saves! Jesus Saves! Spread the tidings all around. Jesus Saves! Jesus Saves! Spread the news to every land, highest hill and deepest cave. Onward still our Lord's command. Jesus Saves! Jesus Saves! ....Wow! That's why we are here!

And to bring me back to reality - the last song was How Great Thou Art and I know the chorus and sang along in Mongolian! ....Then sings my soul my Savior God to Thee. How great Thou art!

So I sat in my living room having my own private worship service. The biggest choir and the most enthusiastic praise team could not have worshipped God more than the praise that came from me. Not just worshipful thoughts. Not just worshipful words. Not just worshipful songs. My soul blessed the Lord for all His benefits (*Psalm 103*) and sometimes I clapped my hands in time to the music. Sometimes I raised my hands in worship. Most of the time I just sang and wept.

You can call it the end of depression, hormones, fanaticism, Jenny being weird - whatever. But when you come to the full realization of God's awesome love and provision for you - especially in the dark times - then you will understand the overwhelming need to worship and thank God for His tender care.

Another good week! Hal and I each got a year older. Thankful to be healthy and able to serve the Lord in this place.

Chapter Eleven

READY FOR TAKE OFF

March 19, 2000
Tests of Various Sorts

    This was a week of testing. We had our big test at school. All of us passed - not with straight A's like we wanted but very respectable, thank you.
    Thursday Hal and I had a special lunch with our teachers so we didn't come straight home. Dennis and Egi had a meeting downtown, so Charlotte came home alone.
    She found their front door damaged and open and items missing from their apartment. They lost all the cash they had, some jewelry and a cassette player. It is very upsetting to feel so violated. It is only stuff and obviously stuff is not important to any of us or we wouldn't be here, but it is still very upsetting. We are thankful Charlotte did not catch the thieves in the act because she could have been hurt. The police are concerned that the thieves will return because they left a lot of stuff behind - like cameras and computers. They have repaired the door and hopefully strengthened it to make it harder for forced entry.
    Then Saturday afternoon our landlord was here doing some repairs so I went to the food market by myself. Just as I started to leave the market, I ran into Dennis. He had just finished buying food so we walked out together - talking as we went. As we

rounded the corner of our building, a young boy (maybe nine years old) brushed against me and it felt different than a normal brush. I pushed back - almost instinctively. He ran like a jack rabbit. I looked down and the zippered pocket of my jacket had been slashed. The remainder of my food money was sticking out. Dennis tried to find him, but of course he had disappeared. It made no difference. He didn't get any money. I wasn't hurt. I am thankful he only cut my jacket. I am thankful Dennis happened along. If I had been alone, the kid might have been bolder in his efforts - like knocking me down. I am so thankful for God's protective angels. I feel them all around us!

Kevin, our missions treasurer in the States, said "God must be getting ready to do something big there in Mongolia because the devil is really putting up a fight!" I pray that it is so! We have been here almost eight months and had one minor incident of pickpocketing on the bus. Otherwise we have not felt threatened in any way. Now in one weekend, each of our families has been tested. So the really big test was not Wednesday in class. It was Thursday and Saturday in life!

Here is another of my silly writings about this not-so-silly topic.

March 20, 2000 - Heaven
Guardian Angel Appreciation Week

Setting: God entering the Guardian Angel Division of Heaven to meet with Bubba, Division Supervisor.

God: Hey, Bubba, how's it goin?

Bubba (getting very busy with paperwork hoping to discourage conversation): Same old. Same old. Those Christians are keepin' my troops busy as usual.

God: All of a sudden I started receiving a lot of prayers from Christians thanking me for their guardian angels. The surge of thanksgiving seemed so curious. Then I noticed in the Lifestyle section of the Heavenly News this morning that this is Guardian Angel Appreciation Week. I've never heard of that. Who set that up? (Like he didn't know!)

Bubba (looking sheepish like an angel with his wings clipped): Well, sir, I'm sure Hallmark will pick up on this soon.

God: Oh you are right. I'm not worried about Hallmark missing an opportunity. I was curious about how it came to be.

Bubba (having regained his composure and feeling more confident): Well, sir, there's National Secretary's Week and National Pet Your Dog Week and National Petunia Week and Lord knows what else. Well, I mean... YOU know what else, sir. It just seems appropriate that guardian angels have their week also. Don't you think?

God: I'm not opposed to this. Your troops certainly deserve a lot of credit and most of the time people are unaware of the work your angels do for them. I just wanted to inquire about your methods for promoting this new appreciation week. Others have spent literally years developing an awareness of secretaries, petunias – whatever. And here in short order, it seems you have the whole world appreciating their guardian angels. I'm wondering if I should move you into the advertising department (known to most of the world as Gospel Spreading Department).

Bubba (looking worried once again): Well, actually, to be perfectly honest (which I know sir you highly condone) to launch Guardian Angel Appreciation Week, I just had my troops rest for a few minutes this past week. Nothing really drastic happened. I made sure that we lost no Christians, but I thought it might be good for the program if Christians had a heightened awareness of their guardian angels.

God: That's an interesting approach.

To the Ends of the Earth!

Bubba: Take for instance the Johnsons and Carrells down there in Mongolia. They have always been fairly appreciative of the work of my department.

God: Yes, I know. I receive their thanksgiving often and they have so many prayer partners! I get requests for their safety all the time – around the clock! There are women who wake up in the middle of the night to go the bathroom and they pray for the Mongolian Mission Team while they are awake!

Bubba: Well, my theory is that anybody willing to go to Mongolia is a good candidate for an experiment. So I tested them this past weekend. The Carrells were never left alone but their angels did let up on watching their apartment and it was robbed. We made sure Charlotte did not walk in on the thieves in action. So, sir, we kept your servants safe. We just let their stuff be plundered so they would appreciate us. And the Johnsons…well we just stepped back from Jenny a little bit and that kid slashed her pocket. But my troops were right there all the time. The kid got no money and Jenny wasn't hurt. But I can say with assurance that these two couples now are very aware of the work of my staff.

God: Very innovative, Bubba! And I thought you were all muscle! Are you sure I couldn't interest you in spreading the gospel to the ends of the earth?

Bubba: No, thanks. I'll leave that to the missionaries – like the Carrells and Johnsons.

God: OK. But next year for Appreciation Week, let's try a special calendar or a mass mailing or something. I'm not running short on grace or peace, but there's no sense in scaring the missionaries needlessly.

Bubba: Whatever you say, Lord.

Afternote: Exactly one month after these events, we began to conduct our church services in a separate rented facility. We felt certain that the thief who stole from Dennis and Charlotte had been attending Bible Study in their home. This incident reminded us of what we already knew. Our homes must be a safe haven in this difficult place. Our attendance at church began to increase. Kevin was right - God was getting ready to do something big!

March 26, 2000
Something Good About to Happen

I know how astronauts feel! I've seen movies and documentary films showing the astronauts strapped in and the rockets rumbling - ready for take-off. Thousands of pounds of thrust quivering beneath them must be exhilarating! Being here in Mongolia with all the power of the creator of the universe rumbling beneath us is awesome! We just feel like something good is about to happen! (Wow! That would make a good song title, huh?) You just can't imagine the feeling of expectancy that we have!

Saturday morning I had the opportunity to teach a small group of women. Although I was able to introduce myself and give a few opening sentences in Mongolian, the actual lesson was taught through a translator. What a thrill to share the beauty and splendor of God's Word to ladies who are hungry to learn! I long for the day I can teach in their language!

Late August 2000

Bill and Rosie (pastor of our sponsoring church and his wife) and Harold (a friend from Florida) arrived on Friday. That morning Biaraa asked if he could come over that evening to ask Hal some questions. We were hoping they were spiritual questions but for all we knew, he could be asking to borrow a hammer.

So the first evening our guests were here, our neighbors came over. And sure enough – it was no hammer he was asking about. He and his son wanted to be baptized on Sunday. Even though there were three preachers in the room, he wanted to ask his questions of Hal – his friend and neighbor. Dema translated for him. Hal answered all his questions (and did a very good job) and asked him if he was saved. He and his son both professed to know Christ and from the looks on their faces and from their recent actions, we believe them! They just beam and Biaraa is witnessing to his parents and friends. He wants to play guitar for our worship services. They are both so very eager!

As soon as we walked into our apartment in August 1999, I felt like it was "right". At first I thought it was because it was a little cleaner than the other apartments and it had nice wallpaper. But women can never fully explain why something feels a certain way so I didn't even try. Hal just accepted my feeling and we moved in.

Well, just a couple weeks later, we met Dema next door and learned that she and her daughter were Christians. She asked us to pray for her husband and teenage son and that her whole family could worship together which is very unusual in Mongolia. We did – and continued to pray for her family for the past year. At Christmas we invited them here - and Biaraa heard the Christmas story as I told it to Egi's children. Then at Easter, both Biaraa and Bilgoon (the son) came and heard the resurrection story. We never pushed, just always remained friendly. All our interaction was in Mongolian because Bilgoon only speaks a little English and Biaraa can say "hello" in English.

Now their entire family is worshipping together. What a wonderful answer to prayer! Did I have faith when I prayed that first year we were here? Well, maybe a mustard seed's worth. Do I have faith now! Yes! Maybe two mustard seed's worth! Was it happenstance that we rented that apartment? No way! That was part of God's plan!

Can it get any better than this?

On Sunday, August 20, 2000 we had our first baptizing service with five people baptized. What a glorious day! We were only touching the ground occasionally as we left that service! I asked our friend Harold if it could get any better than that and he (wisely) said in his slow southern drawl "Well, Jenny, I wouldn't limit God if I were you! It just might get better!" (And it did!)

Russian Spoken Here

Biaraa learned that Bill had been to Russia several times and knew the phrase that means "Praise the Lord" in Russian. Biaraa speaks Russian. As soon as Biaraa came up out of the water after being baptized, he looked at Bill and said "Praise the Lord" in Russian!

God always has a better plan!

> *For my thoughts are not your thoughts, neither are your ways my ways, saith the Lord. For as the heavens are higher than the earth, so are my ways higher than your ways, and my thoughts than your thoughts. Isaiah 55:8-9*

When we were still at Martinez and Egi was attending there, I thought how wonderful it would be for Egi to be baptized there at Martinez. How special that would be for our sponsoring church. I prayed for that to happen, but it didn't.

As the time drew near for Egi to return to Mongolia, I realized that maybe it would be best for him to be baptized in Mongolia as a witness to his wife and family. I prayed for that to happen as soon as we arrived, but it didn't.

Well, God always has better plans for us than we have for ourselves. When will I ever learn that?!? In August 2000 Egi was baptized along with his wife Naara – with his children, father-in-law and sister-in-law observing. So much better than either one of my earlier plans! Thank you Lord for not answering all of my prayers!

Do you know of a town with no church at all?

We had a good time with our guests. We tried to show them the very best Mongolia has to offer – which isn't a lot – but the best we have. We visited Egi's sister who lives in the ger their family was raised in. We had a picnic on the ground by the river. We had Mongolian food at a restaurant in the small town where Egi was born and raised - about 20 miles east of Ulaanbaatar. It appears to have no church. 25,000 people. No church. My heart ached. Please pray that we can start an outreach in that town.

We visited the State Park about two hours east of Ulaanbaatar and I even rode a horse! An old Mongolian man came up and asked if we wanted to ride a horse. I agreed to ride if I didn't have to "drive". So this man got me on one horse and took the rope and got on his horse. As we trotted off he said (in Mongolian) "Say goodbye. We are going to Ulaanbaatar!" I'm not very good at language school, but I clearly understood what he said. Of course, I protested that I only wanted a short ride and he grinned a big toothy grin and kept trotting. (Why is it everyone picks on me? Even total strangers in a foreign land!) It was fun and we only went a little ways! Charlotte did the same thing until he had her horse jump a ditch and then she was ready to get off.

Church in a Bar

Saturday late afternoon we went to the church facility to clean it for Sunday services only to be told that we could not have church there on Sunday because they were installing marble tile on the stairs. The landlord offered to let us use the large space downstairs – the bar. With very few options at that late hour, Hal said yes.

Sunday morning we found that they had cleaned the bar really good. It didn't even smell like alcohol. They had set up 40 chairs – facing the windows instead of facing the bar. A small table served as a pulpit. We had a fellowship planned after services so four small tables along one wall worked nicely. They didn't turn on the disco ball – which we appreciated.

During the services a woman came but she was late and did not want to disturb the services. (Hey, we are meeting in a bar. Nothing would have disturbed us!) But she stood outside the door and listened to the sermon. When we finished, as we ladies started getting the food set out, she came in. Bill began to talk to her and witness to her. She was saved! Standing right there in a bar – after church services were over – while we were putting out food and people were talking! Just goes to prove once again that the posture of the heart is far more important than the physical posture or surroundings.

Rich Heart Baptist Church

Some people attending church need salvation. Some need to come for baptism. Pray with us for a rich harvest. Speaking of rich. We now have an official name – Byan Zoolh Baptist Soom. That means Rich Heart Baptist Church. This section of Ulaanbaatar is called the Rich Heart District. We didn't know that when we moved here. Only after we knew enough Mongolian to read a neon sign in our neighborhood did we learn that. Anyway, we decided that would be a really good name for our church – even if we move to another area of town.

So our hearts are full and we are excited to see how God is going to move in this place. How privileged we are to be here at this time!

It's that time of year when…we have the loudest thunder I have ever heard!

I Don't Know What I'm Gonna Do!
September 3, 2000

If it keeps gettin' better and better Oh Lord, I don't know what I'm gonna do! (A line from an old Southern Gospel song.)

This morning we had the place filled for services! We brought in extra chairs! Had a first-time visitor. The lady who was saved last Sunday came again and asked very good questions after services. She is from a Buddhist background and wanted to know what things she had to do now that she was a Christian. She wanted to know if she needed to light candles or say certain prayers at certain times of the day. Dennis shared the glorious freedom we have in Christ – how there is nothing for us to do but accept the completed work on the cross. What a joy to see her hunger!

After services Baigalmaa (a college friend brought by Zuula – our neighbor) was gloriously saved! She is the one who recently asked "What do I need to do to be saved?" She went to the countryside for the summer as is the Mongolian tradition. We gave her a New Testament to read while she was away. This was her first Sunday back in Ulaanbaatar. Her first words (with tears in her eyes) were how thankful she was that Zuula brought her to church to hear God's Word!

This is how it is done – each one bringing one!

Chapter Twelve

MEMORIES OF A YEAR

August 5, 2000

One year ago today we woke up stiff but refreshed after spending the night on an antiquated train jostling through the green countryside. We looked out the window to get an early morning glimpse of our new home – the land of our calling – Mongolia. The train ride was exciting but nothing compared to the ride ahead!

In the early days, God was making things happen so fast, it made our heads swim. Then we had the whirlwind of getting settled. School began and after the rush of arriving, we fell into the long, hard task of learning Mongolian. The romance of coming to the mission field soon wore off and each day we set about the task of living and learning. What a rollercoaster ride!

Some days I was flush with confidence that I would soon be rattling Mongolian with the best of them. Then suddenly I would plunge downward emotionally – convinced I will never speak this language. I've always tried to be a stable person – not a victim of erratic mood swings, but this past year has been one wild ride! We realize that our goal to be fluent in one year is totally ridiculous so we are returning to school. Our greatest longing remains unchanged - to minister to these precious people in their mother tongue.

We witnessed a beautiful autumn which we didn't fully appreciate at the time. We survived the Siberian winds of winter. We didn't get blown away with the horrible dust storms of spring. We didn't wilt with the short but intense heat of summer. We have come to love the clean blue skies, the puffy white clouds, the dramatic bolts of lightening and the thunderous roar of summer storms, the deep green of the hills, and the brilliance of the sun which shines almost every day – even in winter.

God has given us a special love for these people. I never had a particular fondness for Asian features before but either these people are very beautiful or God has done a beautiful work in my heart. (Or both.)

I've learned to buy food in a market with unrefrigerated meat laying out with flies crawling on it. I no longer stare aghast at a car loaded down with naked sheep carcasses going to market. I enjoy the rhythmic klip, klop of a horse-drawn cart going by on the street below. I've become quite good at taking effective sponge baths when we have no hot water or no water at all. We have finally found an exercise program we can stick with – walking and stair climbing – everywhere we go. I've learned to cook with the products I have available. I've learned several scarf tricks for keeping warm.

I no longer face a long patch of slick ice with as much fear and trepidation although I still prefer the welcome crunch of snow under my boots. I can dart across a busy street, and wait in the middle with cars whizzing by in both directions without my heart pounding like it did when I first arrived. I don't get nearly as embarrassed as I used to when Mongolians laugh at my attempt to speak their language. It still brightens my day to coax a Mongolian child to not just stare at my foreign face, but to smile and return my wave.

But those are not the important lessons I have learned in the past year. I could write a book just about the things I have learned about God and His care for us. I've learned the joy of living out there on the edge – where the gospel message is fresh and new and we sense an urgency to work quickly for the night is coming.

I've learned that homesickness is not a terminal disease. With everything in my life changing, I've come to appreciate anew the unchanging character of my God! I've learned that when I am in the lowest valley, His Word can comfort me. When I think I will die if I don't get to see my kids, He gives me the strength to get through the day. When I am simply too tired to continue, I can wait in His presence and mount up with wings as eagles!

I've learned that you can worship very effectively without a big church building, dozens of people, musical instruments and complex programs. There is no more beautiful sound than a dozen unaccompanied voices lifted in songs of praise! Dennis preaches the simple message of God's love. Does it get any better than this?

When I am at my lowest times, I get on my knees and ask God to refocus my thinking – away from my pain and toward His work. When I get tired of dealing with life here, God brings someone into our services who has never heard the gospel in their entire lives – and then I remember. We didn't come here for the exciting adventure or the change of pace. We came here so these people can hear that Jesus loves them. That's why I'm studying Mongolian. That's why I'm making all these adjustments in my life. That's why I've abandoned my children and family and friends. That's why I have an ache in my soul – for the salvation of Mongolians. Thank you, Lord, for entrusting that burden to me.

It's not the way I thought!

I thought saying goodbye that last night in California would be gut-wrenching, but it wasn't. God granted that wonderful peace that passes all understanding. I can't explain it. How could parents leave their children behind and have peace? It's not natural.

I thought Mongolia would feel very strange and foreign, but it didn't. Even though this place was strange, it felt like home from the very beginning. I can't explain it. I just know this is where we belong right now.

I thought establishing a comfortable home in this faraway place would be difficult, but it wasn't. God has provided everything we need and lots of niceties on top of that! I can't explain it but sometimes I actually feel pampered in this developing country.

I thought language study would be challenging but no more difficult than other projects I have tackled in the past. I was wrong. It is far more difficult than anything I have ever undertaken. I can't explain how difficult it is to think in a new way, in a new order, with new grammar and new words and sounds.

I thought culture shock was something that happened just a few weeks after you arrived, but it isn't. Culture shock can wash over you at any time for any or no reason. I'm not sure you ever completely get rid of culture shock as long as you are in a foreign land.

I thought the first winter would be horrible – dark, dreary and depressing, but it wasn't. Yes, it was cold, but we managed just fine. I actually like winter here.

I thought it would be a while before we were able to minister to Mongolians, but I was wrong. God has brought so many people across our path. Some speak English. We use translators to minister to the others. What a blessing!

I thought we would exist on rice and mutton and potatoes all year, but I was wrong. In the winter, our selection of vegetables is rather limited, but the rest of the year, we have a nice variety to choose from.

No, it is not the way I thought at all! It is far better! Thank you Lord!

Chapter Thirteen

NORMAL IS GOOD

Mongolian Entertainment

Often the TV cable goes out, but who needs TV? We have a show right outside our window. I'll see if I can describe it for you.

The street in front of our building is wide enough for two cars plus a couple of feet to spare. When cars park at the curb, there is only one lane for traffic. When cars face each other head on, someone has to back up. Everyone knows that. The trick is who is going to back up? I've been told that the biggest vehicle has the right-of-way. I think it is the driver with the loudest horn and the most stubborn will.

Several times a week (daily?) cars meet head-on and sit there for five minutes (I'm not exaggerating!) and blow their horns and motion for the other one to back up. Sometimes other drivers who are backed up behind, get out of their cars and go up to try and reason with the lead drivers (I should say "sitters" since no one is moving). Eventually someone gives in. Usually by then there are ten or more cars backed up in each direction.

One night we had extra excitement. One car which I shall call New Car (NC) meets head-on with a Big Old Russian Truck (BORT). All the other cars behind them in both directions back up so it is really a battle of the wills between NC and BORT. After several minutes BORT laboriously backs up – not enough for NC to get by but just enough so that NC can pull into a vacant parking place at the curb – allowing BORT to get by. (Ingenious driver!) After BORT moves forward, several cars backed up behind him go also. NC remains at the curb (probably still stewing over the fact he merely got to park and not go.) Then cars that were backed up behind NC make a beeline for the now clear road – honking to tell NC to stay at the curb because they are comin' through!

Just a little ways down the road there is a car parked at the curb and a car has stopped beside that car and turned his lights off (LO). Remember with two cars in the roadway, there is may be two or three feet in the middle. Well one of the cars backed up behind NC hotdogs it down there, gunning it all the way. He either didn't see LO or he thought his car was only three feet wide. Bang! Yep, he hits the front fender of LO.

So the two drivers get out to inspect the damage. In the meantime NC has pulled away from the curb where he has been sitting all this time – and decides he must go forward NOW! He sets on his horn and flashes his lights and carries on big time. Finally the hotdog driver and LO driver get in their cars and drive away. It seems that nothing is ever done when there are crashes. I have even seen people hit by cars and if the person can hobble away, they do nothing.

What did I learn from this incident? (1) Horses would never do this. They graciously go around each other. (2) Maybe bringing Mongolia into this century was not totally wise. (3) This noisy scene is a lot less annoying when there is no cable than when the window is open and we are trying to hear something on TV.

October 1, 2000

Another wonderful day in the Lord's House! God *hath dealt bountifully with me. Psalm 13:6b.* We had church, then we had a fellowship meal, then we piled into a rented van and drove across town for our baptizing service.

What a great day of worship and fellowship! We used butane hotplates to reheat soup. Add rice, bread, dessert and beverage – and we call it a meal. The people love to sit around and talk. Then

16 of us rode in a van that was designed for 12. No problem! We have close fellowship!

What a joy to watch the Lord add to our number! Can't wait to get to church each week to see how God is going to work.

A Secret Letter to Craig

October 2000
Dear Craig:

I used to try to write near your birthday every tear. Then I just wrote whenever I could. The past year I have been very negligent in writing to you. Of course, since I am writing secretly, you don't know that. But I do have a really good excuse – being on the mission field and a full-time student and all! But no excuse will ever be good enough to explain why I don't have time for my children.

You turned 21 in August. Wow! How time has flown! Seems like only yesterday that I sleepily woke up to see your father's face and asked if the baby was OK. That was the single most important question. He grinned and said "yes". Then I asked if it was a boy or a girl. Your dad told me it was a boy. Those were the old days when you didn't know the sex of the child until it was born. Can you imagine?!

I asked if the baby was pretty. And in typical fashion your father said "he looks like a worm". And that is how you got the nickname Worm. You not only looked like a worm but when we held you, you squirmed around and snuggled close – just like a worm! Even at two years of age, you would tuck your arms inside so they were between your body and mine and that is how you wanted to be held! "Tucked" I called it.

Anyway, what an exciting ride you have given your father and me! Never a dull moment – even now – 21 years later. This past year you gave us the wonderful thrill of telling us that God was calling you to preach. What a joy! I remember back when you were about eight years old, I said "Craig will either be the leader of a rock band or a preacher – a dynamo at whatever he chooses to do!" I was so thankful that you were saved at a young age – before sin could leave its horrible scars on your life.

Dad and I are so pleased with your decision although at the time of this writing, you are driving us nuts with trying to drop out of college. We just want the very best for you and hate to see you throw away an education that could serve you so well in the future. Our churches needs well-educated pastors to lead them. Whatever you decide to do, we pray that you are one of those great leaders of the future.

At this time, I still haven't heard you preach. I still can't figure out why no one has been able to capture your preaching on video. It hurt so bad when I learned that the video of your first sermon was blank. It just seems so little to ask – that I get to see and hear you preach, but so far I haven't. God has helped me deal with this disappointment. I know someday I will hear you and I know I will be proud.

I continue to pray for my second daughter-in-law that at the perfect time, she will find you – or you will find her. I know God has a very special girl that He has been preparing for you – for many years now. I have prayed for her regularly for over 21 years now. I know you are getting anxious to meet her also.

I can't even start to explain how difficult the past year has been. I never dreamed I could go this long without seeing you – and survive. But with God's grace I have. I think of you so often. When the boy next door plops his arm around his mother's shoulder, a pain shoots through my heart. I don't regret coming to Mongolia. I know it is God's will for our lives right now and it has been a terribly exciting journey, but that doesn't ease the pain of separation! I just pray everyday that our coming here and leaving you behind has not scarred you in any way. I know our leaving was harder on you than on Chris – who has Stephanie to lean on. I just pray that it makes a stronger Christian out of you.

"I love you" doesn't really communicate the full measure of feeling that I have for you. Coming to Mongolia has made me appreciate more fully the love I have for people – most of all my children. Oh what I would give to simply sit down and have a chat with you – not that I have anything terribly important to say. Just talk – about nonsense or heavy issues – whatever. Someday we will do that! And what a precious time that will be!

Love you lots, Mom

History from a Different Point of View

One of my teachers told me this week that when she was a child in the early 70's she was afraid of Americans because the news said Americans were horrible for dropping bombs on North Vietnam and later Nicaragua. Of course, being a communist country, they got their news and opinions from other communist countries. She said now she realizes that Americans are good people. Interesting to hear about history from a different viewpoint.

Lessons in the Countryside

My language helper took me just outside of town to learn some country words. She talked to me all the way through town, pointing out buildings and asking me questions. Her friend who was driving was highly entertained by my Mongolian. I'm glad someone finds this struggle entertaining.

We left the paved road and headed for the wide open field. Mongolians are not bound by roads – nor hindered by the lack thereof. We stopped near a little stream. After discussing and naming everything within reach and discussing everything far away, we walked to the stream.

My language helper said (in Mongolian – her only language), "you go across the stream". It was too wide to jump in one leap. I would have to step on a dry rock in the middle. Not a problem for me, but I knew exactly what was next. She wanted me to help her across! She has lost one leg in an accident. She gets around fairly well on her artificial one but she still had to lean on me a lot to walk on flat ground. I could just see the two of us soaking wet in the middle of the stream with sprained ankles or broken artificial leg!

First I pretended to not understand her Mongolian, but you see, the eyes never lie! If I really do not understand, I can never convince my teachers that I do. And likewise, in this case, I understood clearly what she was saying but when I tried to act like I didn't, she knew better. Finally I abandoned ignorance as a defense and said – "No. We can't do this." She is a very gutsy lady. Anyway, she gave up disappointedly and we discussed things from afar. (This is one of the very rare occasions that I actually won an argument with a Mongolian!)

People are all alike.

Before we left the stream, she bent down and got a handful of water and put it on her hair. Not sure exactly what that meant, but I shared with her that my grandmother used to always wet her hair when she got near a stream. Her face lit up and she said that my grandmother was a good woman. Aw! Connections happen at the most unexpected times.

Horse with boy. Boy with horse. Whatever!

A flock of sheep and goats came by. We discussed their size, color, gender and eating habits. One goat was blue. Honest! Either that is a strange breed or a bad hairdresser did a job on him! We watched the sheepdog work the animals. Amazing! A boy on a horse was overseeing both the animals and the dog. The way you say "a boy on a horse" in Mongolian is "horse with boy". I said it backwards and said "there's a boy with horse". My language helper and her friend laughed for five minutes! I guess they were picturing a boy carrying a horse on his back. I didn't think it was all that funny, but when you are outnumbered (which we always are), you laugh along with them.

Excuse me! That is NOT clean!

Then she showed me dried dung and explained how country people collect it and burn it for fuel. Then she took me to a pile of fresh dung and told me it was clean. Well, there are some things that transcend language. One is facial expressions. My mouth said "OK" in Mongolian but my face was screaming "No Way!" They both laughed again and called me a City Woman. Guilty as charged!

Sugar Daddy

Buildings in Ulaanbaatar always have a guard. You probably think of a young man in a uniform but here they are usually women or old men. They do provide some level of security.

At the school we attend, there are several guards who each have a 24 hour shift. One of the ladies has a ten-year old daughter named Sanjidmaa. Other than attending school, she stays with her mother on her shift. She is a very engaging young girl and we became friends. OK, actually she tolerates me but she loves Hal! Hal buys her juice for breakfast and gives her cookies from our snack. She gives Hal an extra 30 minutes of language drill before class two mornings a week. She also reviews his homework and corrects his pronunciation. About the time Hal finishes school, she is walking to school. So Hal walks her there each day and she rattles the whole way, explaining things to him like only a ten-year old can.

She knows just a little English. I tried to teach her a new term - Sugar Daddy. I don't know if she understands the words but she definitely understands the concept.

Unexpected Blessings

Sometimes blessings come in unexpected ways and sometimes we are blessed in ways that we didn't even know we needed blessing.

Sanjidmaa told Hal that she would be singing at a church event. So of course, Hal and I said we would attend. I don't know if we were missing children's events (after so many years of that) or if we were preparing for our grandchildren's events or what.

Anyway, we braved a cold wind and maneuvered a taxi ride and a long walk – most of the time clueless of where we were - and asked directions of people and tried to understand their Mongolian. But we found the place and how glad we were that we made the effort!

Over 200 children sang praises to God with the energy and enthusiasm that only children possess. Hal and I have worked in children's ministries for over 20 years. I started leading children's music when I was about 14 years old, so of course, my love of children's gospel music goes way back! I didn't even realize how much I missed children's music. To hear "If I Were a Butterfly" sung in Mongolian – well, it was great – to say the least! Hal and I just sat and grinned. We were the only pale faces in the crowd but we felt perfectly at home! I thank the Lord for bringing into our lives an element that I forgot I was missing!

Familiar Sounds

When the wind blows, a piece of sheet metal outside our building rattles loudly. When we first moved here, I always noticed the sound. Now it is like the steady rhythmic breathing of a sleeping child. Unnoticed but unconsciously pleasant. Just part of life here.

Late at night a train comes into Ulaanbaatar. In the summer when the windows are open, you can hear the rhthymic clatter of the rails. Not loud enough to be annoying. Just the comforting sound of home.

You sell me food. I have food for you!

Two of our regular vendors at the food store came to church today. That made Hal and me very happy. We invited them over a month ago, but we don't nag every time we go to the store. Then yesterday one of them mentioned that the store was going to be closed on Sunday. We asked if she was coming to church and she said "yes" and pulled out of her pocket the map we gave her over a month ago! So she had not forgotten our invitation!

My boring life is an asset!

I have been writing a daily journal (in Mongolian of course) as part of my homework this year. My life is so boring. There is seldom anything new to write about. School, homework, dinner, sleep - repeated everyday except Wednesdays and Sundays when church is added to the mix. There are only so many ways you can write the same thing over and over!

So I began to venture abroad in my writing. I mentioned that we were watching the Middle East crisis on the news and that I found it interesting because the conflict began back in Bible times. The next day the teacher wrote a response in my journal that she did not understand and would I explain. So the following day I told her the story of Abraham. On Friday she said instead of my usual daily journal, she wants me to write about more interesting things – like Abraham. Boy, do I have some stories to tell her! And yes, they are far more interesting than my daily life!

There are so many opportunities here! I just pray that we don't overlook a single one of them and that we have the strength and wisdom to present the gospel to every seeking soul.

Normal is Good

I would love to tell you that life on the foreign field is just one exciting day after another, but in reality it is like anywhere else. Much of life is simply normal, but considering all that could be going on, I am thankful for normal. No illnesses. No injuries. No robberies. No emotional upheavals. No failed tests.

I used to play this game with Hal back in the States. Just think, honey, today we didn't lose our jobs, didn't have to visit the emergency room at the hospital, didn't spend time at the funeral home, our children are not behind bars, the bank didn't foreclose on our house and we didn't wreck the car. The dog is still healthy, the kids are still ornery and we are still married. Life is great!

Defrosting the Freezer

For some of you older readers, this will be a walk down memory lane. For younger readers, it will serve as a glimpse back into history.

Some may wonder what on earth we do all day here on the mission field. Sure we tell you we are in school four hours a day, have three to four hours of homework everyday and living here is hard, but in our small apartment, how hard can hard be? When I try

To the Ends of the Earth!

to describe why I have no time, it is not a single thing. It is a combination of many tasks – none of which are easy or efficient. This is a description of just one of those tasks – defrosting the freezer.

Determining the need: When you have to use a knife to pry your frozen foods out of the freezer - that is a hint you need to defrost. When you have to lean your entire body against an item to get it into the freezer – that is a hint. When your freezer can only hold half the normal capacity – that is a hint. My freezer's normal capacity is three ice trays, two lbs. of hamburger and a small roast. So now you understand why it is important to defrost regularly.

Getting ready: Put on the tea kettle and get a bath towel. Now you may wonder how bad a task can be if it includes a cup of tea and a hot bath. Well, honey, that water is not for tea and that towel is not for you! Turn off the refrigerator. If you can't read the dial (like my refrigerator is Russian), just unplug it. Leaving it on while you try to defrost is like trying walk up a "down" escalator. You can expend a lot of effort, but you won't make much progress.

Next you remove all the frozen foods and all the food out of the refrigerator. You may ask why you empty the refrigerator when it is the freezer you are working on. Well, these refrigerator freezers are combined, so when the two inches of ice melts from the freezer, it drips down……you guessed it…..into the refrigerator. The sound is reminiscent of rain on a tin roof – but not nearly as pleasant. Place the towel on the floor to help sop up the water that runs out.

Begin: Place a pan in your frost-encrusted freezer and then gently pour boiling water into the pan. It will cool quickly so repeat this step many times. You need to learn the elbow trick which is how you keep the spring-loaded freezer door from popping up, dousing you with water. You will probably spill water on the floor carrying it from the freezer to the sink. Not to worry. You always have to mop after you defrost. It is like a law.

As the ice begins to melt, you can use a butter knife to pry chunks of ice away from the freezer compartment. Now some may have heard about the trick of using a hair dryer to defrost. For some reason that never works for me. It seems the hot air thaws my frozen food on the table before it thaws the chunks of ice clinging to the freezer. So I use hot water.

With half my body inside my refrigerator, I careened my neck to see how to pry loose ice that had filled the two inch space between the wall of the refrigerator and the wall of the freezer. That is where they put the freezer coils which provides a perfect pocket for ice to form, but it is a real challenge to get it out as it curls over the top of the freezer compartment. Anyway, in this less than comfortable position, with water dripping off my elbow, a thought flitted through my mind. I wonder if Martha Stewart would stencil flowers or stars on the underside of her freezer – for special moments such as this? You laugh, but that makes about as much sense as …. Oh never mind! The thoughts of Martha Stewart trying to survive in Mongolia provided all the mental stimulation I needed for the next 30 minutes as I fought with ice that looked like it could sink the Titanic.

Finishing up: After you win the battle with the ice, you wipe down the freezer and refrigerator. Wash the vegetable bins which are always too large for any sink so you will drip water on the floor near the sink – to match the wet floor near the refrigerator.

Instead of simply returning everything to the refrigerator, this is a good time to combine the two half jars of mayonnaise and toss out questionable items. Refrigerators are really quite magical appliances. They change the color of everything. Green things become brown. White things become green. Red things become black. Etc.

I read somewhere that humans like to eat all color of things except they don't prefer blue. For some reason if you put out four bowls of punch that are identical except for the color – one red, one green, one yellow and one blue - no one will touch the blue punch. Well, I didn't find anything blue in my refrigerator (packaging doesn't count), but I sure found a lot of other colors that I wouldn't touch. Even in a developing country where I frequently eat things I cannot name, I will not eat un-nameable things from the back of my refrigerator!

So with everything wiped off, use your best organizational skills to try and make more room in your tiny refrigerator. Your new ROP (Refrigerator Organization Plan) will probably last at least a day or two.

Wring out the wet towel that is sopping wet in front of the

refrigerator. Mop the floor. Close the refrigerator door – and enjoy the private satisfaction of a job well done – because no one can tell that you have done a thing for the last hour and a half!

Afternote: We know have a frostfree refrigerator. Praise the Lord for small blessings!

Black Market Treasures

Sometimes we go to the Black Market. There is nothing illegal about it. That is just the name given to it. It is like a gigantic flea market. I do not like flea markets or garage sales. God has a strange sense of humor! I hate to shop, Hal hates the cold, and we both like things to be done efficiently. So God sends us to Mongolia where we have to shop and search for everything, cold weather lasts six months a year and absolutely nothing is done efficiently! Some days we find humor in all of this. Other days…well, there are other days.

Here in Mongolia your best chance of finding stuff is at the Black Market. Most of the stuff is new but some of it is used. At least it is all in one place so you don't have to traipse all over town looking for something.

The Black Market is always crowded - even when the ground is frozen solid and slick. You must be extremely careful and don't put anything in your pockets that you are not willing to donate to the pickpockets who work the Black Market. When we first arrived in Mongolia, we visited the Black Market to find household items for our apartment. I swore that was my one and only trip and that I would never go back. Well, I guess I have adapted. I have been back a couple of times and it doesn't even bother me anymore! Now, I'm not saying I'll ever become a fan of garage sales but here in Mongolia, it is the best way to find stuff.

So we went to get some fabric for curtains to keep the cold out. Even though it was a toasty 10 degrees above zero, we were smart enough to wear the full complement of gear and thankfully we did! There was a slight breeze but it felt colder than when we have been out in weather 22 degrees below zero. I guess I had a firsthand lesson in wind chill factor.

We got there early and not all the vendors were set up so we were just wandering around and I came across a vendor with Singer sewing machines – hand cranked or treadle. It reminded me of grandma's old treadle sewing machine in Arkansas. But most of these machines were hand cranked probably because the treadle cabinet takes up too much room. Out in the countryside once I saw a woman sitting on a blanket outside her ger using a hand cranked machine to sew. I wonder if the antique dealers of the world have ever thought of coming to developing countries to find old items? Maybe it is just as well that they have not. What would these people do without their machines?

So about the time I think this place is really coming of age - I see something like the sewing machines and I am reminded that despite cell phones and computers, this country is years behind the rest of the world.

Our trip to the Black Market was a Big Find Day for me. I found an oven pan! (It doesn't take much to make me happy.) Ovens are a relatively new thing for Mongolians - who usually cook over open fire or on a two-burner hotplate. Although ovens are becoming more common, no one has figured out that you can't put the plastic-handled pans in the oven. I had not been able to find a pan so we bought a frying pan and removed the plastic handle and I used that in the oven. That day at the Black Market, I found a porcelain pan. What a thrill!

Icicles, Potato Masher and Mexican Food

A Big Week! I saw icicles dripping, Hal found a potato masher and we located the only Mexican restaurant in town!

We had two foot icicles hanging from roofs since November. Friday afternoon as I walked home from school, I heard the sound of dripping water and looked and the icicles were dripping! I knew what that meant! Spring was on the way! It got up to 25 degrees above zero F! That is mighty close to breaking the freezing point. Also I don't have to break icicles off my mop before I use it. (Although the deck is enclosed, during the winter, things out there freeze.)

Spring was in the air!! You cannot really enjoy spring until you have endured a Mongolian winter.

I had been looking everywhere for a potato masher since we arrived. Saturday Hal and Dennis went to the Black Market to get some home repair supplies and what did Hal find but a potato masher! No more mashing potatoes with a hand egg beater!

I had been craving Mexican food for months. We had seen an ad in the English newspaper about a Mexican restaurant advertised as the only one in town. (I believe them.) Hal looked for it twice but couldn't find it. Finally he told Egi if he could find it, he would buy him lunch there. Egi found it promptly. (Food is a great motivator.)

By the way, lest you think Hal is a total nitwit, only the main streets in town have names (maybe six or eight streets total). None of the buildings have numbers. So addresses read like "Located in the former Adam's Club (like we know where former businesses were located), south side of Peace Avenue (the main drag) not too far from the bus stop west of the State Store." In fact those are the exact directions to the Mexican Restaurant. It was well-hidden back in a residential area, but with Egi's help, we enjoyed Mexican food.

It must be spring!

It seems that spring brings more snow than winter did. Sometimes we have snow flurries almost everyday. We got the notorious spring winds we had heard so much about. As I write this, the wind is howling outside. This morning as I walked to church, I met the building guard outside. I made the mistake of saying "Sain baino uu" (Hello. How are you?) When I did, I got a mouthful of grit which I felt all the way to church - until I guess I finally swallowed it. In the future when the dust is blowing, I think I'll stick to nodding my head only.

Rotary Dial Phone Replaced

We got a new telephone instrument. Got rid of the old red, rotary dial phone. Now we have a modern phone with buttons! Even a speaker so we can both talk to the kids at the same time (just like the good old days!).

UPS Arrives

It is strange the things that bring comfort. UPS recently started delivering here in Mongolia. When I first saw the familiar brown van, it brought a smile to my face.

Lord I'll get it down. You please keep it down.

I had a real test of my culture skills. For years I have read of missionaries being faced with such situations. When I have been faced with something like this before, I was with others and I could politely partake and it not be noticed that I was not wholeheartedly embracing the event. But this time there was no hiding in the crowd.

After my practice session with my language helper, she said she had fixed food for us to eat because she gets tired of eating alone. So of course, I had to stay and eat. I am accustomed to buuz and horshol and Mongolian salads. But she had fixed country food - what the people in the countryside eat. I wouldn't hurt her feelings for anything in the world. So I overlooked the difference in hygiene standards in the kitchen. I had the task of setting the table and I confess I selfishly chose the cleanest spoon and fork for myself. Note I said "cleanest" not "clean".

I knew I could handle the boiled mutton (it really wasn't bad) and the rice, potatoes and carrots looked friendly enough. The one item that caused me concern was a milky soup made from a product that could best be described as very strong cheese. They melt it and then add a glob of yellow lard that looks like candle wax. So there were globs of yellow grease floating on the top of the milky mixture. She made sure she served me plenty of the yellow grease because she said it was good for me.

She served me up huge portions and we sat down to eat. I asked her if I could pray and she said yes. I offered a traditional blessing with my lips but my heart was praying different words. "Oh Lord, please help me eat this and keep it down." I wanted to be gracious and not offend her. I had shared the gospel with her. She had come to church. She was my language helper. We had become friends. I believe she will be saved someday. I refused to let my personal preferences get in the way.

The mutton, rice, potatoes, carrots and bread were really quite good. The white soup stuff – well even if I hadn't seen the black hair floating in it, I think I might have struggled. But I did manage to eat eight or ten big spoonfuls – from the side of the bowl opposite the hair. It had a very strong taste - similar to mare's milk only hot and thick. (Oh yum!) We discussed (in Mongolian of course) each food item – how it was fixed and the health virtues of each. I told her it was the first time I had eaten the white soup. I described the taste as interesting and strong. I used the word bitter but she corrected me with a Mongolian word less sour than bitter. OK. Whatever.

I did it. I ate most of my food and was a gracious guest. I asked her if now I would be able to speak good Mongolian. She just laughed.

Thank you, Lord for grace to get through all the situations I find myself in.

Sourdough Saga

After living in the San Francisco area for 29 years, sourdough bread had become a part of our lives – easily obtained at any grocery store. About a year after we arrived in Mongolia I realized that I was very hungry for the taste of sourdough bread. The very best bread you can buy here has very little flavor or texture.

So I tried my hand at making sourdough bread for the very first time. I found a recipe for a starter on the internet. I mixed it up thinking – I usually throw out things that smell this way and here I am caring for it and feeding it twice a week! It said to fix it in a large glass jar. Well, I didn't have one so I used the biggest plastic jar I had. I wisely decided to put a pan under it and sure enough it began to rise (more like "take over the kitchen"). Thankfully, my curiosity kept me checking on it. After a few minutes, I divided the mixture into two jars and still it rose.

The first step was to leave it out overnight. I made it through that stage with only a small mess when each jar ran over. Then into the refrigerator it went. Three days later it was time to feed it again and then let it rest. Well, here we go again with stuff oozing over the edge. I remember a movie once about a blob of stuff that took over the world. I was afraid I would wake up the next morning and see sourdough starter oozing down the hall toward our bedroom!

It was a pain dealing with two jars of starter (complicating the feeding process) so I went to the store and got the biggest glass jar I could find. It was pickles. I bought them and emptied the contents into another plastic container and used the jar for my sourdough starter. Then I started looking for recipes that used large quantities of pickles.

Saturday Hal made chili so I made sourdough bread to go with it. I was wondering. When you make bread, you knead it and let it rise and then you punch it down and let it rest. Why does the bread have to rest? I am the one who did all the work!

Oh my goodness! That was the best Sourdough Bread I have ever eaten! I've never tasted better at any restaurant in San Francisco. It was worth all the fuss!

I made Sourdough Chocolate Chip Muffins. Egi happened to be here when the muffins came out of the oven so he taste tested them. He gave his approval. (Like he would dislike anything with chocolate in it!) I made Sourdough Drop Biscuits and they were very good also. Usually my biscuits can double as paperweights or hockey pucks. But these were very light. The list of sourdough items went on and on – for which I was thankful since I had a lot of starter – which I fed twice a week. I wonder how pickles would taste in sourdough bread?

My kids probably wonder why I never cooked like that when they were at home. It was too easy to buy. Sorry, kids. You will have to visit Mongolia to test Mom's new culinary skills.

God's Glitter

One Saturday we went out to do errands and it was snowing lightly. I love walking when it is snowing. It is so gentle and soft coming down - like a whisper. I waited outside while Hal went in to exchange money and I happened to turn and see the sun shining through the snow. It looked like glitter! I think maybe God was sprinkling white sparkly glitter on this part of His "picture".

One prayer that is always answered!

Through the years I have had many prayers answered. But one prayer that is always answered – affirmatively – usually immediately – is when I ask God to give me an opportunity to witness. And when I ask, I also always ask for the courage to carry through and He gives that also.

This week I had the privilege of speaking to two people about Christ. One is my language helper and the other is one of my teachers who has attended church once. Both were in Mongolian. Both were simple and rough due to my language handicap but I believe God's Word will not return void – even when coming from the stammering lips of someone speaking in their second language.

> **It's that time of year again when...** The sound and feel of snow crunching under your boots is wonderful!

White as Snow

I'm learning so many things here in Mongolia. This week as I was doing laundry (which brought washing to mind) I found myself singing (and later belting out the words accompanied by handclapping):

> Are you washed in the blood? In the soul-cleansing blood of the Lamb?
> Are your garments spotless? Are they white as snow?
> Are you washed in the blood of the Lamb?

I had sung that song all my life but now I knew how white snow is! The mountains around Ulaanbaatar are so white they look like crystal. When the sun shines, it is brilliant and when the sun goes down, it seems like the snow kind of lights up the night.

It snowed all day yesterday. The forecast predicts snow four days this coming week. Of course, they forecasted overcast skies for yesterday so I'm not sure we can depend on their predictions.

A Reasonable Facsimile Thanksgiving
November 26, 2000

Hope Thanksgiving was special for all of you. We had a reasonable facsimile of Thanksgiving. Thursday and Friday were regular school days. Saturday I fixed chicken, dressing, mashed potatoes, green beans and pumpkin pie and sourdough bread of course. Chicken substituted for turkey because there is no turkey to be had in this country at any price. Today I saw a huge blackbird that I think could have served as our turkey if we could have caught him.

The cornbread dressing was really good. I was so happy to find celery at one special produce vendor downtown. The cornmeal came in the Action Packer from the church last March. The canned pumpkin and evaporated milk I got in Beijing last July. Anne brought me the pie pans last summer. So after many months of gathering and hoarding, we had Thanksgiving. Dogi joined us and loved everything. She is real easy to please! After two years, do you know how wonderful celery smells cooking? Or pumpkin pie? Well, trust me, it smells real good.

Things are certainly changing here quickly. At the market on Friday I saw for the very first time – vanilla, chocolate chips and a variety of spices. I am grateful I have all those products already though. One 12 oz. bag of chocolate chips was $6.50! Vanilla was outrageous also. But until now these products could not be purchased at any price. Of course, we may not see them again until next year. We used to have a nice selection (that's four or five kinds) of Campbell's soup – cream of celery, cream of chicken, mushroom and tomato. Now there is none. The "soup train" has not been to Mongolia in a while.

If anyone thinks life on the mission field is all spiritual – 24 hours a day - then they haven't been reading my writings for very long. There's a lot of humdrum to deal with. This week we have fussed with a leaking kitchen sink drain – all week! The plumber keeps coming out and fiddlin' with it. (They don't believe in replacing parts!) The really exciting part is – I've been reporting this to

To the Ends of the Earth!

the landlady in Mongolian. The first time I called to report the problem, I did my best – on the phone – no body language – no pointing – no jestering. We're talking pure Mongolian here. I hung up and Hal said "Did she understand?" I said "I don't know. If a plumber shows up in a little while, she did." Sure enough! A few minutes later a plumber rang our bell. An exciting moment in my language learning.

The thieves come up empty again. Praise the Lord!

One Friday Hal and I were on a very crowded bus. All the buses were crowded so we really had no choice of the matter. I know crowds are where pickpockets work the most so I thought I was alert. I had my book bag off my back and holding it in my hand so the bag was beside my leg. I sensed something and looked down and a man was fingering one of the zipper compartments. All that was in that compartment was Kleenex. I gave him an annoyed look and moved away to another crowded section of the bus.

Not until Monday did I discover that my bag had been slashed the full length from top to bottom. Thankfully, all he felt was my language books. I was carrying my camera that day to take some pictures at school. It was in the very middle of my bag with books on both sides. It would have broken my heart to lose my camera. So I am thankful he didn't get anything. But it is tiring to have to always be on guard and it is annoying to get hit even when you think you are on guard. The joys of living here! Now I hug my bag like it is a lost child just found.

Interesting sights: I saw a jackhammer breaking up a section of sidewalk on Friday. First time we have seen one here. Usually that work is done manually by pick and shovel. It was drawing quite a crowd of onlookers.

How do you dig holes in frozen ground?

It appears a fence is going to be installed around a lot near our apartment. With the ground frozen solid, the way they dig holes for the posts is to build a small fire where the hole is to be dug. After it burns a little while, they put the fire out and dig the hole before the ground freezes again. In a few places, they had to build a second fire down in the hole until they could finally reach dirt instead of ice. The fence has not gone in yet but there are black holes around the perimeter at set intervals.

It's that time of year again when... A hat is a necessity – not a fashion statement.

Mornings are now about 20 degrees below zero F. During the day it warms up to zero or a little above. Our apartment is still quite cool. Thankfully I don't have a thermometer for the house – only the one on the outside of the window. If I knew the temperature in here, I would probably really be cold. I can put on enough clothes to keep warm. But it's hard to do anything with gloves on. You think my typing is bad without gloves, you should see it with gloves.

It's that time of year again when... hot tea and hot coffee were made for days such as this.

My Downsitting

Wednesday night after Bible Study I was walking along with my neighbor and Hal. It was very dark. And suddenly one of my feet was more anxious to get home than the rest of my body. In other words, I slipped on the ice. I have slipped many times (like daily) but this is the first time I have gone completely down. It was so fast. One minute I was walking along upright and the next I was scooting along like an ice cube skittering across the kitchen floor. I am so thankful that I didn't twist, sprain or break anything. I'm a little sore but that's all. I landed on the padded side of my body.

Thou knowest my downsitting and mine uprising.
Psalm 139:2

OK so maybe that is not the downsitting the scripture is referring to. Whatever!

It's that time of year again when...you better know exactly where your bus stop is because the windows of the bus are frozen over. (Not fogged. Not frosted. Frozen). This morning when we got up it was 29 degrees below zero F. It warmed up today to five below zero. And the really cold weather doesn't start for another couple weeks! So we may be seeing some temperatures we have never seen before. But in answer to the obvious question. Really cold is really cold. Ten below doesn't feel much different than two below. Praise the Lord for hot drinks, hot soup, hot radiators and hot water!

Weekly Fall Report

I fell down again. Maybe I should just sit down and scoot where I want to go. Ya think? On Wednesday, it was pretty warm so I put on my autumn boots. (Big mistake!) I didn't need winter boots for warmth but I sure needed them for traction! I had to maneuver a small hill. My boots didn't have enough traction. I broke one fall by being close enough to a metal fence to grab ahold. But another time there was nothing nearby and I went down square on my backside. It jarred my whole body. I think it "packed" the Mongolian in my head. Amazingly – and thankfully – I wasn't hurt. I didn't even get sore like the other time when I fell.

The other day Hal came in and said he had found me some new shoes. I thought he was serious. I should have known better. He said he saw a horse-drawn cart and the horse's shoes had big spikes – like nails – on the bottom – to keep the horse from slipping. He said he wants a pair for me.

He will keep the feet of his saints. I Samuel 2:9

One of our teachers indicated to Dennis and Charlotte that she and her husband might come to church. You know, I've often thought – it would be such a marvelous testimony of God's power if we Christians were brilliant linguists – learning Mongolian faster than any other student. But maybe we show more of the love of God by sticking with it even when it is very difficult. The teachers all know we are learning their language for one reason only – to share the gospel. And this has to be a labor of love. There is no amount of money or prestige that would motivate us to endure what we are enduring!

> **It's that time of year again when...**going outside is a ten minute process to get on your gear and staying inside in soft clothes is heavenly!

Strangers are not invited in

The highlight of my week was a conversation I had with Amaglan. She said that she will not invite a stranger into her home when they knock on her door. Nor will she invite a stranger into her heart. But she said every time she reads the Bible, her eyes are opened. She is slowly learning about God and His love for her. I believe very soon, she will be opening the door of her heart to the Lord – who was a stranger to her until the past year. What an honor to introduce people to Christ!

I remember in my Stateside life, I often felt sorry for missionaries. They gave up so much. Boy, was I wrong about that! I should have been envying them for the life they lead! On the mission field there are blessings and emotions that even with my prolific fingers, I simply can't capture in words! Maybe this is the *meat that you know not of. John 4:32*

> **It's that time of year again when...**If you really like pain, just take off your gloves for a few minutes.

What if this would be the year?

With the regular and frequent trouble in the Middle East, it seems Christ's second coming must be very near. A song has been ringing in my heart for weeks. If you know the melody, sing along:

To the Ends of the Earth!

What if this would be the year that Jesus comes?
The year that we've been waiting for so long.
We'd have so little time to get our lost world won.
If this would be the year that Jesus comes.

This may be the year!

Transportation

Public Transportation includes a few new buses which give new meaning to the word crowded. There are electric trolleys that are ancient and slow, but have come to be like comfortable friends to us. Then there are the old buses. Think about the oldest bus you have ever seen and add 20 years to it! We call these tour buses. They have see-through bottoms to observe the landscape below. (There are holes in the floor.) Some are like an amusement ride (bucking like a wild horse and careening around corners). They are air conditioned especially in winter (holes in the windows). Some offer nature indoors (snow comes through the roof).

There are lots of cars ranging from Mercedes (for political dignitaries) to Russian jeeps to cars that contain so many different parts, they long ago lost their identity. There are few roads in Mongolia therefore sturdy vehicles are needed to go cross-country. Even in Ulaanbaatar, the roads are in such terrible condition, vehicles get beaten to death.

Taxis are everywhere in Ulaanbaatar. In fact any car going by is a potential taxi. You simply hold out your hand and if the person stops, you use your best Mongolian to tell them where you want to go. You crawl in and either you practice your Mongolian on the driver or the driver practices his English on you. In America this would be a very foolish thing to do, but here in Ulaanbaatar, it is a way of life.

Most of the time we use the most common and reliable form of transportation - walking. The Mongolians call is "using my two brown horses" – referring to their legs. OK, I guess I would have to say "using my two white horses". Anyway, we often walk two or three miles a day – carrying whatever we bought or whatever we are taking with us.

Every day we claim the promise in *Psalm 91:11 & 12: For he shall give his angels charge over thee, to keep thee in all thy ways. They shall bear thee up in their hands, lest thou dash thy foot against a stone.* We have truly been borne up in the hands of our guardian angels!

Weather

The best way to describe the weather in Mongolia is extreme and extremely variable. This is a landlocked country wrapped by China on the east, south and west and by Russia to the north. So there is no large body of water nearby to temper the weather. There are four distinct seasons but in any one day we can experience several seasons.

Winter is the dominant season lasting from October until March. Although snow is common throughout the winter, it is often too cold to snow. We had the new experience of having our breath collect in our eyelashes and then freeze. God helps us through the winters and we praise Him!

Springtime in Mongolia means wind and dust storms. Even though the snow just melted, the ground is very dry. The temperature can drop 10 or 15 degrees in one hour. One day it was in the 20's and snowing and less than a week later it was in the 70's and sunny. Summer is very hot but very short. Autumn brings the only rain of the year – a welcome relief to the extremely arid conditions the rest of the year.

The thing we have all noticed the most about the weather is how dry every season is. In winter, they sweep the snow instead of shovel it. In autumn it can rain one day and the dust be blowing the next. It seems the ground just absorbs any moisture like a sponge. All of us fight problems like cracked cuticles, split heels and rough, itchy skin.

More dramatic than the dry climate is the spiritual dryness we find here. Mongolians who have been deprived of God's Word for decades are so thirsty for the living water. Teaching here is a joy! It seems that *Psalm 63:1* was written about Mongolia. *O God, thou art my God; early will I seek thee: my soul thirsteth for thee, my flesh longeth for thee in a dry and thirsty land, where no water is.*

We remain your representatives – delivering the living water to the ends of the earth.

Freedom

When you hear the word democracy, you probably think of a place just like America where people are free to do anything. Although Mongolians are freer than ten years ago, they are not free. Many things have them bound.

The history of oppression continues to haunt them. Americans always have the attitude "We can do anything! No one can stop us! We are the best!" That comes from 200+ years of success and accomplishment. Just as our history colors our attitudes and thinking, the many years of repression colors the attitudes and thinking of Mongolians. We see it in subtle and not so subtle ways.

Communist thinking continues to permeate this place. A friend asked me if it was really true that in America you could travel to other states without government permission. I told her yes. We can visit other states (even Mexico and Canada) or we can even move – without the government's approval. She was amazed! I told her that is called…freedom! The government still controls the lives of people here and they have come to accept that as normal. And the chaos and inconsistency of laws and law enforcement is shrugged off as just the way it is. The years of oppression have made Mongolians docile and willing to endure things that Americans would never stand for.

Things are different now!

Things were very different when Mongolia was under socialism. There were no poor people. Everyone made the same wage. There were very few thieves. In the countryside people would leave their homes unlocked. Alcohol was rationed so there were few alcoholics. There were not a lot of cars clogging the streets and polluting the air. There was no dissatisfaction because they had no way of knowing about life in the rest of the world. Travel was restricted to other communist countries and the media was controlled and news was filtered. The government provided everything that was needed - from food to medical care to building and street maintenance. There were not a lot of worries or decisions to make. The young people were told what profession they would pursue and the education was provided along with a job afterwards. Neat, clean, simple, controlled.

Some old people long for the old days under socialism. But many prefer a democracy even though times are hard and a lot of bad things have happened - alcoholism, poverty, prostitution, crime, pollution, dissatisfaction, corruption…and the list goes on. One precious Mongolian friend said despite all the bad things, she was thankful for the democracy for one reason…..she heard about the God who loves her and sent His son to die so she could have eternal life.

We are thankful that we have the opportunity to be here. *Psalms 86:9 reads: All nations whom thou hast made shall come and worship before thee, O Lord; and shall glorify thy name.* Yes, Mongolians deserve the opportunity to come and worship.

Chapter Fourteen

PROSPERING IN HEALTH

Beloved, I wish above all things that thou mayest prosper and be in health, even as thy soul prospereth.
3 John 2

Often we are asked what we do for medical treatment here in Mongolia . For simple things, we treat ourselves with medicine we brought from the States. For serious things we will get out of the country. Medical care here is far below the world standard so we pray we never require any invasive treatment.

An American doctor toured several local hospitals and said he saw medical procedures that were used at least 50 years ago in America. When we first arrived we met a nurse from England who came to Mongolia to train nurses. She said she had more training as a nurse in England than the Mongolian doctors have here. She had to teach nurses to wash their hands between patient exams!

She said that she was looking at the chart of a cancer patient and asked why the patient's stomach had been removed when the cancer was not in the stomach but in other organs. She was told "We couldn't do anything about the cancerous organs so we just removed the stomach so the patient would feel like we were trying to do something." The patient eventually died.

Mongolian hospitals feel more like prisons than hospitals. The buildings are in need of repair with dark hallways and less than sterile surroundings. Mongolians are often hospitalized for several weeks for a condition that would be treated on an out-patient basis in the States.

Please pray for the Mongolian Mission Team that we remain healthy so that we can continue the task of sharing with these precious people the One who *was wounded for our transgressions, he was bruised for our iniquities: the chastisement of our peace was upon him, and with his stripes we are healed. Isaiah 53:5* That healing is far more important than any medical treatment anywhere in the world!

Are you thankful for good hospitals?

There are some aspects of Mongolian life that I don't think I will ever become accustomed to. Hospital care is one of them.

Dema and I went to see a lady who had visited our church - a young mother who has had repeated problems with her female organs undergoing six surgeries in less than three years.

In most Mongolian hospitals all the hospital staff provides is medical care. Dema said if no one brings a patient food, the hospital will give them something to eat but it is very bad. So it is best if food is taken to the patient. Our friend had trouble keeping food down so Dema made a mild soup and I made homemade bread and finger jello.

The first floor of the hospital had a huge waiting room with chairs. We walked up to the third floor where our friend was. There was another large waiting room with absolutely nothing in it. I have been in cleaner bus stations! Paint was peeling. Floors were dirty. Windows dirty. Depressing is the only word for the place.

It was a cancer hospital so all of the patients were very sick. I could see down a wide hall that was equally depressing. Patients were hobbling along, holding the wall but there was no handrail. Not a wheelchair in sight. Dema said patients must walk out into the hall to the common restroom. There were no doctors or nurses in sight. If someone collapsed (which some of them looked like they could), I'm not sure who would find them. Occasionally there was a faint whiff of the smell of alcohol but mostly it didn't smell like a hospital.

Finally Dema saw a nurse and told her who we came to see. About five minutes later our friend slowly walked toward us with great difficulty. She was extremely thin and weak. When I hugged her, I felt like she would crumble in my arms! She wore a mask for protection from germs (a good idea). Visitors can never go into the patient's rooms. Patients must always come out to meet their guests and get food that is brought to them. They keep a bowl and spoon in their room for food – washing it themselves of course.

If a patient cannot come out to the waiting room, they cannot have visitors. Since there was not a single place to sit, we went to the window and our friend leaned on the windowsill while we talked a few minutes. (Now I always take a folding stool for the patient when I make hospital visits!) I prayed and Dema translated. I prayed that God would give the doctors wisdom to diagnose and treat her condition – a common prayer when someone is sick. But here I think that might take a huge miracle!

Our friend then returned to her room carrying the food we brought. She wanted to bring Dema's thermos back to her. I was watching and saw her slowly walking back toward us with the empty thermos. I told Dema "why don't you go get that so she doesn't have to walk all the way back here." It pained me to watch her walk! Dema did as I said without hesitation. When Dema reached her, our friend said "if the nurse sees you, she will be angry!" Thankfully the nurse didn't see Dema. Hal says next time I go, I should do that fetching and if I'm stopped, just play the dumb foreigner role. Not a difficult part for me to play!

The doctor said our friend should stay in bed so I felt guilty that she walked down to see us. But she said she was so happy to have visitors because no one comes to see her. (Afternote: She joined our church the following year.)

I was sick, and ye visited me. ... Inasmuch as ye have done it unto one of the least of these my brethren, ye have done it unto me.
Words of Jesus in *Matthew 25:36 and 40*

December 10, 2000
Just Needed a Reminder I Guess

Life is hard here in Mongolia. Every day is begun with prayer that we will remain safe. This week we had an extra reminder of how fragile life is.

Hal woke up with one side of his face paralyzed. I think this would have been frightening if it had happened in the States, but it seems scarier here. God had it all in control – always had – always will. There is one American doctor here in Ulaanbaatar. We were able to see him by noon that day. He diagnosed Bell's Palsy and had the medicine on hand that Hal needed. Praise the Lord! We were so thankful it was nothing more serious!

So a little something extra to deal with. Hal now has a lopsided smile, his speech is sometimes difficult to understand, he has blurry vision and he is having to learn to eat and drink all over again. We understand that usually these symptoms clear up within three months. Of course, we are hoping for a quicker recovery. We have places to go, things to do and people to see. We have heard from prayer partners around the world. What a blessing!

Afternote: Hal completed the regime of medicine and several weeks of acupuncture and fully recovered. Praise the Lord!

Patience 201

In August 2001 Hal injured his shoulder. The American doctor was out of town so the Mongolian doctors put him in a grotesque cast that kept his arm away from his body. He was almost helpless. Couldn't cut his food. Couldn't put on his socks. Couldn't tie his shoes. Couldn't button his pants. Couldn't take a shower or bath. (He was real nice to me during that time.) I guess Hal and I failed our last lesson on patience so we are getting a repeat course.

After two weeks, he began therapy. I went with him to one of his massage treatments.

Medical Testing – Mongolian Style

As we walked into the medical facility, a young boy was sitting on a rock with a makeshift holder containing several test tubes each filled with blood. Around each test tube was a paper probably identifying the person whose blood was in the test tube. The amazing thing is there was no stopper or cap on the test tubes. Just open vials of blood taken to be tested. If you have ever walked these dirty streets, you know that there is no way dust stayed out of those blood samples. Maybe their testing equipment is not sensitive enough to notice a little dirt.

Power Tripping

Hal went upstairs for his treatment while I sat in the lobby. It was dirty as are all medical facilities here. A man walked by with a mask over his face. I didn't know if the mask was to protect him from my germs or protect me from his germs. By the looks of the man, I suspect the latter.

An old woman served as doorkeeper. There was a padlock on the door and she locked it between each person coming or going. I don't mean hook the lock through the bolt. She clicked it locked between each person even though she was standing right there and even though she saw people (like doctors or nurses) coming who needed to go out. So it was lock it, unlock it, lock it, unlock it - continuously.

When the lobby got a little crowded, she threw some people out in no uncertain terms. I expected to be next but somehow I escaped her purge. When she occasionally walked away into the other room, no one went in or out. She had the only key. Everyone just waited until she returned - sometimes five minutes. She was obviously the BOTL (Boss of the Lobby) and enjoyed that power to the max!

Caught Up on my Praying

After about five minutes of observing the BOTL, I spent the remaining 30 minutes or so in prayer. First I thanked God for

America - specifically American medical facilities. (Have you done that lately?)

Then I thanked God for our safety since we have been here. None of us have required any serious medical procedure. It would only take a moment of inattention and we could be hit by a car. Or a wrong move on the ice could do serious damage. Or we could pick up some disease. But God has spared us all of that for which I am very thankful.

Then I prayed for our continued protection as we work here. And I threw in a little prayer that the building would not catch fire while the doorkeeper was gone with the key. (God answered that prayer. I got out OK.)

Yes, going to the doctor helps me catch up on my prayer life.

What are they serving today?

When Hal first went to the trauma hospital with his shoulder, they x-rayed it and put it in a cast. Hal didn't think it was broken but he knew he was in pain. As he sat there watching, he noticed they were casting injuries that he thought strange. Like a small puncture wound was put in a cast. A skin abrasion was put in a cast.

A few days later we visited the American doctor and he said Hal probably had a pulled muscle - not a broken bone. Although the cast was overkill, it wasn't doing any damage. Hal told him that they seemed to be casting every injury the day he visited the trauma hospital. Dr. Brad smiled and described to us the same principle that we use for food inventorying.

If a load of canned beans arrives in Mongolia, we have canned beans for weeks. Then we won't have beans again for months or years. He said the doctors had probably just received a fresh supply of casting material so that day they were doing casts.....for everything! Don't you love it!? I'm thankful they had not received a new shipment of surgical instruments the day Hal went in!

Chapter Fifteen

RELIGIONS OF MONGOLIA

Thou shalt have no other gods before me. Exodus 20:3

In our monthly reports, we did a series of articles about the various religions and the spiritual condition in Mongolia.

Shamanism

The original religion of the Mongolian people was shamanism which is the worship of nature. They believe there are many gods – the sun god, moon god, fire god, etc. For example Chinggis Khaan (spelled differently by the Western world but the same great leader who united the various nomadic Mongol tribes into one nation) went to a mountain and asked for the heaven to help him and bring him victory when he went out on conquests. There is no book of teachings but beliefs are handed down from one generation to the next. There are many taboos associated with shamanism which have become a part of Mongolian culture.

As you travel through Mongolia you see ovoos – a mound of rocks with a pole in the middle with blue cloth tied to it. Various items are placed at the base of the rocks – food, money, bottles and other objects. Mongolians walk clockwise around an ovoo three times to bring good luck. If there is a single tree growing apart from other trees, it is also decorated and worshipped.

The central figure in shamanism is the shaman – a person who claims to have special spiritual powers to cure illness and talk to the dead, etc. They have religious services and go into trances. Although shamanism is considered a primitive religion, it is still practiced by some in Mongolia today.

In Romans 1:25 the Bible talks about shamanism – *(they) worshipped and served the creature more than the Creator.* Please pray for us as we tell them about the Creator who loves them – as they are – sinful, disillusioned man.

Buddhism

Mongolia began to follow Buddhism in the 1200's when they were at the height of their power. At that time they had the largest empire in the world – reaching from Korea across Asia to Europe and from Siberia south to Vietnam. They embraced what is called Northern Buddhism or Yellow Buddhism which emphasizes submission and compassion. These beliefs helped outside nations to easily repress the Mongolian people.

Buddhism involves no faith. It is a rational, personal effort to emancipate oneself from anguish and suffering by doing good deeds and thinking good thoughts. It is not a system of faith and worship but a path to enlightenment. They believe after you die you are reborn as another person and your condition in the next life is dependent on your behavior in this life. When you achieve ultimate enlightenment, you reach nirvana.

Buddhists follow the directions on a calendar (like a horoscope) for many of their daily activities. For example, they never get their hair cut without first seeing if it is a good day for hair cutting. They believe in luck and think if they pay the lama to read a prayer on their behalf, they will have good luck. Or if they turn a prayer wheel (with a prayer inside), they will have good luck.

In the 1930's the communists conducted a purge of Mongolia – destroying Buddhist temples and killing or exiling all lamas and forbidding the people to worship. When Mongolia gained freedom in 1990, Buddhism began to flourish. Some politicians would like all religions banned from Mongolia except Buddhism.

Christianity

From the 1930's until 1990 Mongolia was a communist state. People were forbidden to worship in any manner. School children were taught that religion is like a narcotic – habit-forming, a bad thing, a crutch. So one entire generation was raised with athiestic, Darwinistic teaching.

Mongolia's democracy brought freedom of religion. For the first time in many generations, Mongolians could hear the gospel. After 60 years of a spiritual vacuum, this is a fertile harvest field with many people hungry to hear God's Word. What a thrill to watch the faces of adults as they hear the wonderful news of God's love – for the very first time! What a privilege to be the messenger! Many souls have been saved for which we are thankful.

Some Mongolians think if they accept the historical facts about Christ and if they read the Bible and go to church, they become believers. We tell them that devils believe in God too. (Check out *James 2:19*) It takes more than head knowledge about Christ. It takes more than going through the motions of reading the Bible and going to church. Christianity is accepting what Christ did for us on the cross and having a personal relationship with God through the perfect sacrifice of His son.

Of course, freedom means anyone can come here. One sect offers free trips to America for new converts. We know people who have signed their paper in order to study in America for a year. These people are desperate to catch up with the modern world and this seems to be an easy way! We have been asked if we offer such trips. What we have to offer is far better than a trip to America!

Silver and gold have I none; but such as I have give I thee.
Acts 3:6

Taboos

The Mongolian culture has many taboos originating from

To the Ends of the Earth!

shamanism and Buddhism. Here are some I find interesting.

> You never whistle inside a house because you will call the devil.
>
> If a newborn child is taken outside, Mongolians put a black smudge mark on its forehead to scare away the devil.
>
> You always say children are ugly. You never say a child is cute or pretty. It will make the devil want it.
>
> You always take a different route home from a funeral or graveyard than the way you went – so that evil will not follow you home.
>
> If you are traveling on a bumpy road, you never say it is a bad road because you might anger the road god. (Trust me, there are lots of Mongolian roads that qualify for this!) Yes, we have a problem with saying nice things about bad roads and saying a newborn baby is ugly! Go figure!
>
> You never extend your feet toward the fire. Fire is sacred.
>
> It is bad luck to trim your fingernails at night. This may have originated many years ago before good lighting was available. They didn't want fingernail clippings in their food.
>
> Mongolians don't like to be praised in their presence. It will make the devil want them. If you praise them, they will deny it.
>
> If you speak about bad things (like death), it will make it happen. Mongolians do not like to deliver a negative message. They will talk all around an answer rather than just say "no". You can imagine how annoying this is to

Americans who just want the answer to the question.

You never talk about a child before it is born nor do you buy anything for the baby. The day a child is born the father goes to the store and buys clothes and supplies.

Taboos are so binding! We are here to share the truth and the truth will make them free. *John 8:32.* Please pray for us as we labor in this field.

Greatest Ache

The greatest ache in a missionary's heart is not the pain of going years without seeing family and loved ones. It is not the stress of being far from everything that is familiar. It is not the deep-seated longing for more churches to give so that the needs that you see so clearly on the front line can be met. It is not the painful yearning for more workers in the field although you weep when you stand in towns of several thousand people with no church – of any kind.

No, it is none of those. The greatest ache in a missionary's heart is the overwhelming desire to see souls saved. That longing is so strong it is an actual pain that brings tears to our eyes. But to see a person with their face etched with the worry and stress of facing eternity with no hope – accept Christ and smile with the joy and confidence only Jesus can give – that special moment makes all those other pains and inconveniences vanish. To know that you will see that person in heaven – and they will be there because you shared the gospel....well, there's no other feeling like it in the world! If every church member in America could experience that moment, there would be no lack of mission funds. There would be no lack of workers for the harvest. There would be no dry eyes.

Oh Father! Give us a new, clear vision of our mission. Wash our eyes with tears so that we can see precious souls as You see them.

They that sow in tears shall reap in joy. He that goeth forth and weepeth bearing precious seed, shall doubtless come again with rejoicing, bringing his sheaves with him. Psalm 126:5 and 6

Initial Public Offering (IPO) Available
(This segment written by Hal)

Have you ever wished you could invest in a new company and make lots of money? Probably. We all have. After the IPO we can only purchase stock from someone else - usually paying an increase in price over the IPO.

Let me recommend an IPO that you can get into without paying a premium, always has stock available and the return is great. The company has been around for a long time, has a proven record of success and has worldwide operations. The primary work of the company is to spread the gospel to lost souls. How can you invest in the company? Through your local church. Investment is supporting missionaries on the field. Will you realize a return? Guaranteed! You will see souls saved and churches started for the Lord and the best part – the CEO of the company (God) will personally deliver your return in heaven. Have you ever received dividends personally delivered by the CEO?

If you are looking for a place to invest, consider the opportunity in Mongolia. It has a large natural resource supply (souls to be saved). Entrepreneurs (that would be us) are in place ready to work. It needs venture capitalists (that would be you). The company is in desperate need of a factory (building in which to do the work). There is plenty of stock. (Each soul that accepts Christ is a share of stock for you.) You have to hear about an IPO in order to sign up to purchase stock. In this company there is no signing up. You can invest any time – any amount that the CEO lays on your heart – no minimum or maximum. You will receive monthly reports.

Why not invest in something with proven success? There is a guarantee that the company will not go out of existence (*Matthew 16:18*). The CEO is the same as yours and will never change (*Matthew 28:20*). We have already had dividends paid on the investment in the short time we have been operating (souls have accepted Christ as savior). What earthly company can guarantee you ongoing existence, a permanent CEO, and abundant return? None that I am aware of. Will you invest in souls? Will you lay up treasure in heaven?

Worship
(Written in early 2000)

God is a Spirit: and they that worship him must worship him in spirit and in truth. John 4:24

How often I used to say - church was rather flat today because:

1. The pastor was gone and the substitute was not as good.
2. The pastor just didn't seem to preach a very good message.
3. The praise band didn't play. The music seemed bla without them.
4. The choir didn't sing. It just didn't seem the same.
5. The pianist was gone. The substitute needs to practice more. The music dragged.
6. So many people were gone. The church seemed empty.

Here in Mongolia there is no praise band, no piano, no choir. Only the four of us....and God. And we are worshipping! Occasionally the regular preacher (Dennis) has the substitute (Hal) present the Word and you know what? It is ever bit as good as when Dennis preaches. The sermons are right on point. The music touches our hearts. Accompaniment is not a problem – we don't have any. Worship has nothing to do with things. It has to do with the condition of the heart! Too bad I had to come all the way to Mongolia to learn that! Father forgive me. Thank you for opening my eyes to what worship really is.

Challenges We Face

God is working in a mighty way here in Mongolia. These precious people have not had the gospel for thousands of years and now it seems the windows of heaven are opening to them. However, there are also obstacles.

The Buddhists offer tangible things to worship - the touch of their brass Buddhas, spinning a prayer wheel, offering a food offering, etc. Then there are shreds of shamanism still alive in this place.

Some groups offer money and benefits to those who will follow their beliefs. But there is yet one more obstacle - one you might not expect. Christianity.

Recently one of our teachers told us again a story we have heard many times since arriving. In the mid-1990's a couple of young teenage girls committed suicide by jumping off a tall building. They were not associated with any church that anyone knew of but in their pockets was Christian literature that said "If you ask Jesus into your heart, when you die, you will go to heaven - a place of beauty and comfort." These young girls had an extremely difficult life here so apparently they were searching for a way to escape this place. My teacher said she is opposed to Christianity because of this incident.

I explained that these young girls did not have proper teaching. They were given a scrap of information which they did not fully understand. Maybe that is why in the Great Commission in Matthew 28:19-20 the word "teach" appears two times. We are here to teach the "all things" of the Bible. Pray for us as we face these many challenges.

Chapter Sixteen

COUNTING THE DAYS UNTIL FURLOUGH

January 7, 2001
Rollercoaster Days

I've always been a fairly stable person – not given to emotional swings. In order to be a personnel manager for 24 years, I had to be the steadying force in the office. However, even missionaries have ups and downs. I feel just a tiny bit guilty because I seldom write about the downs. There are always plenty of things to write about that are upbeat or funny or encouraging or interesting or weird. I always tell you the truth. I just don't tell you the whole truth. The only guilt I feel is that some may think this is a true, accurate view of life on the mission field – and it is only half the story.

Today started out as a down kind of day because we had only eight people at church. Several of our regular members were sick. One who attends regularly was in the hospital. Others who said they planned to attend, did not come. Some have gone to the countryside for a winter vacation. Others are simply not faithful. They come if there is nothing better to do – just like in America. I always found that annoying in the States and I really find it annoying here.

Dennis reminded us that God is more concerned with the condition of hearts than with the number of people present. How many times I have "worshipped" (yes, those quotes are intended) in a large congregation, but my heart was not in it. So I guess it wasn't really worship at all. Today there was nothing to do but worship from the heart. By 11:30 we had 13 present (with two first-time visitors), but the worship had already begun in our hearts. A song I know says "When I was in the lowest valley, His strong hand was leading me." So true.

Hal fell down on the ice Tuesday and hurt his wrist a little but he is OK now. This was quite a surprise for my "sure-footed as a mountain goat" husband!

If you are not a religious person when you come to the foreign field, it will make you one. This week I had to cross Peace Avenue. It was solid ice – slick and treacherous. The traffic was very heavy (like it is all the time) and there was no traffic light to stop the cars. I stood on the side of the street for probably five minutes before I felt even a little bit comfortable to inch and scoot my way across the icy street. I was praying the whole time "Oh God, please help me get across the street safely." If a car starts sliding out of control, even if they don't want to hit me, they might. And you can never get all the way across the street at one time so you end up standing in the middle of the street with traffic sliding by on the ice in both directions. Prayed up. Paid up. Ready to go up. That's the way we must live!

It's that time of year again when... at high noon the sun is barely above the horizon.

January 14, 2001

What a joy! Today we began Sunday School classes for the adults. Hal is teaching the men and I am teaching the ladies. I recruited some prayer warriors in the States so of course it went really well although teaching through a translator is very different! You don't realize how important rhythm is until you have to teach one sentence at a time. You have to constantly think in two directions. You are thinking ahead to the next thing you are going to say and you want it clear and efficient and it can't be too long. But you have to hold the thought you just said in case the translator asks you to repeat it.

What a joy to finally get an opportunity to teach. And one lady asked to counsel with me afterwards. Joy, Real Joy, Such Wonderful Joy!

And worship service was good. We had more men than women – a unique situation in Mongolia but what a thrill. God continues to bless in spite of our weaknesses!

40 Degrees Below Zero

We had severe cold again this week. One morning it was 39 degrees below zero F. Did you know that 40 degrees below zero Fahrenheit is the same as 40 degrees below zero Celsius? I didn't know that until I lived it.

Although our apartment was warm earlier in the winter, it was quite chilly this week. For those of you who think it is just me and my age – Hal noticed the difference also. We just put on another layer of clothes and used the portable heater. One afternoon while doing homework, I held a hot water bottle to keep my fingers warm.

It's that time of year again when... 15 degrees below zero feels warm!

January 21, 2001

Each one of us has a different sphere of influence. That was proven to me again this week. Hal had opportunity to witness to one of his teachers. I had this teacher last year and she made it clear she didn't want to hear about Christ. Dennis and Charlotte have had this teacher and didn't get far either. But this week she listened to Hal and asked questions. He thinks she will come to church. She did tell one of her friends and he came to church this morning.

Attendance at our classes and church was down this week. Disappointing but we will teach if we have only one student. We had good sessions anyway.

It's that time of year again when... I wear more clothes sitting in my living room than I used to wear to football games in California.

Recycling and Substituting

Last Sunday we had stir fry (beef, peppers and onions) with rice. Monday (taking a tip from Charlotte) I used beef broth (from a roast I cooked recently), added a little potato and carrot. When those vegetables were tender, I dumped in the leftover stir fry and rice. I also had a dab of leftover corn that got added. Voila! Stir Fry Soup. Not bad.

Then I decided I wanted bread sticks. I plunged into mixing up the dough before checking to see if I had all the ingredients. I had about 1/2 cup of milk and the recipe called for two cups of sour milk. I didn't really want to get coated up and go to the market especially since the temperature was already 15 below and dropping by the minute. So I scrounged around and discovered I had some fake powdered cream. I mixed it with hot water but it still didn't mix up completely so I strained it – using the liquid part only. Then I added a few drops of lemon juice to make sour milk. Voila! Bread dough! Not bad.

Cooking in America must be so boring!

It's that time of year again when... your breath fogs into your eyelashes and freezes so it looks like everyone is wearing white mascara.

Be Prepared

Thursday Amaglan made horshol for me for lunch. They were very good – the best I have ever eaten. You have to eat them like Boy Scouts - always prepared ... to wipe the grease that drips off your chin!

Just So Proud to be Here

This week Amaglan asked me when God's birthday was. I told her He had no beginning and no birthday. She then innocently asked me "What did you celebrate in December?" So I got to explain the Trinity in Mongolian to this dear lady who is a practicing Buddhist.

Hal got to explain mercy and grace to one of his teachers in Mongolian. What a joy! I am absolutely certain that our explanations are rough and inadequate but we are doing the very best we can. We are thankful they are asking and we are "just so proud to be here". For those of you under age 50 or for those of you who do not follow country music – the phrase in quotes is the famous opening line of Minnie Pearl of the Grand 'Ole Opry. No, we don't wear price tags dangling off our hats like she did!

OK, so maybe the cold weather has gotten to me – just a bit.

> **It's that time of year again when...**the muscles in your buttocks remain tight while walking – in preparation for when you step on a patch of ice and go slip sliding away.

February 18, 2001

Just three students in the ladies class this morning, but the lesson was as real to me as if I had a roomful. I know I must be faithful over a few before the Lord will entrust to me a large class. I am thankful for the conscientious students who attend. Once again Hal had more men than I had ladies. We are thankful for that also. Mongolia needs strong Christian men.

> **It's that time of year again when...**Ulaanbaatar is shrouded in smoke from the gers and from the smoke belching out from the heating plants. It makes Los Angeles' smoggiest day look clean! Honestly!

Tsagaan Sar

Tsagaan Sar is the biggest holiday of the year in Mongolia - like Thanksgiving, Christmas and New Years all wrapped into one. It is a time for families to get together and honor the oldest family member.

The teachers at school put on a Tsagaan Sar party for the students. It was beautiful! The teachers all wore gorgeous dells. We wore our dells also. They had tables set beautifully and the food was good. Guess who the oldest person was? Yep – it was Hal! He is older than any other student or teacher. He was the guest of honor and sat at the head of the table and was served first. Dennis was second oldest and I was third oldest. Actually I think a couple of teachers are older than me, but they wanted the students to be the guests of honor. So I was really just pinch-hitting for an old person.

They sang songs that were either really beautiful or God has given me a special love for these people (or both). We had a fashion show of dells and then they did traditional Mongolian dancing. A good time was had by all!

On Tsagaan Sar Eve we visited with a family in our congregation. They live in a suburb of Ulaanbaatar in a one-room house. They burn wood to cook and heat, haul water from down the hill, and have an outdoor toilet.

We were honored to be invited as part of the family. We ate buuz, salad, cheese and drank milk tea. They cooked a sheep back and put it in a dishpan in the center of the table. The meat was really tasty. Then they built a round bowl out of hard cookies and filled it with candy and hard cheese. The older men presented us with their snuff bottles. We were expected to admire the snuff bottle and sniff it (or go through the motions anyway) and return it to them in a respectful way. They sang Mongolian songs and were entertained by our attempts to speak Mongolian.

What is that in the bottom of my cup?

The next morning we visited two Mongolian families. As is

customary, we were served milk tea in a small bowl. I sipped along enjoying it until I got near the end and there was a white glob of something in the bottom of the bowl! Maybe it was a hunk of cheese or a buuz leftover from the last person who used the bowl. I decided I had enjoyed enough milk tea.

I'm not a big breakfast eater and to face greasy buuz at 10:00 a.m. after finding a white glob in my tea – well that took a little courage. And there sat Dennis and Hal popping buuz like malt balls! I was going to count how many the guys ate, but math has never been my strength so I didn't!

Wet is cold in the winter.

We visited another home and I sat on the couch. When I stood up and the air hit my backside, I realized my entire bottom was wet. Either I had lost control or I had sat in something wet. Discounting that first possibility, I hoped beyond all hope that it was water – and not a child's failed attempt to avoid the outhouse. It was probably 20 degrees outside – which felt quite warm to us – except for my bottom which was a little chilly until it dried.

We visited the home of one of our teachers. Hal had witnessed to her regularly over the past few months and we were hoping she would come to church. We met her family and ate more buuz, drank milk tea, admired snuff bottles, etc. When one of her relatives wanted to pour a round of drinks for everyone, she stepped right in and told them that we don't drink and she made it clear that her guests were to be honored – despite our strange habits. They toasted us and we smiled. We appreciated our teacher respecting our beliefs.

The homes of these people are stark and harsh, but they are happy. They were together with their loved ones, eating their favorite foods and entertaining foreigners. I guess it doesn't get any better than that!

We met so many Mongolians and our heart ached to win them for Christ. Their lives are so difficult. We can't raise their standard of living, but we can certainly help them gain a mansion someday!

It's that time of year again when...you must dry clothes inside because if you put them on the deck, they will freeze and crack.

53 Days until furlough! Love, Jenny

March 4, 2001

This week I pulled together our slide presentation for furlough. I cried every time I reviewed my work. I told Hal that if I wasn't already called to this field, I would be. He said I cried my way through deputation before we came so he expected me to cry my way through furlough! As annoying as tears can be at times, I never want to become hardened. There seems to be no danger of that!

We had a good Ladies Class this morning. What a privilege! We were studying I John 1:9. I used the story of David to illustrate it. Of the six ladies present probably only one of them had ever heard the story of David. I just loved it! Their look of anticipation brought back memories of the four-year olds I used to teach.

What a great story of how God can use us – even after we mess up big time – if we will only repent.

> **It's that time of year again when...**Spring is such a flirt! Comes on really nice and warm and winks at you – making you think she is going to stick around....then leaves abruptly and the snow and wind return.

46 Days! 7 Weeks! 1 more calendar turning....so many ways to count time!
Love from the ends of the earth! Jenny

March 11, 2001

What a great week!! A soul was saved!

> "It's shouting time in heaven! A sinner once lost is found. It's shouting time in heaven! Salvation has been brought down." (Song by the Hoppers)

God is more real!

You know, it seems like God works in more visible ways here in Mongolia. Does God work in America like this but it is simply not acknowledged? We don't know. When Jesus was here on earth, He did miracles so that people would know who He was. The people of Mongolia do not know who God is and He is revealing Himself to them – in dramatic and visible ways.

One of our teachers told her brother about our church and he began to attend. He needed a job and although he had not yet accepted Christ, he asked God for a job. Within days he got a job that he really likes. He said God answered quickly and provided a good job that he really likes. So then he believed in God and accepted Christ as Savior. Thank you Lord!

I've never been sure if God answers the prayers of unbelievers (other than a prayer of repentance). I still don't know. I do know God is alive and well in this country and revealing Himself to people who are seeking Him.

There is resistance. A member of Parliament said Mongolia has violence because they have allowed Christianity to come in and Christianity is based on the crucifixion – the worst form of violence. Mongolia has violence – not because of Christianity but because they have embraced the very worst aspects of Western culture – horrible bloody movies, prostitution, alcohol and drugs.

Teaching God's Word in the Presence of an Idol

This week I prepared and taught children's Bible stories to my teacher. She loved it – especially the flannelgraph. My teacher asked if I would prepare Bible stories everyday. She likes them better than reading newspaper articles. So do I! I'm preparing for the time we start classes for children at church.

I taught the same Bible story to Amaglan. What a thrill to sit there in her living room – within arm's reach of her Buddha – and teach her about the true and living God! And she asked for another lesson on Monday! She finished reading the book of Genesis that I gave her and asked for the rest of the story.

They didn't know his name.

This week after my Bible story, my teacher was telling me (again) that for the 70+ years under socialism, Mongolians were forbidden any type of religion. She said her parents never heard about God or Buddha. I asked if they believed anything. She said – oh yes. They believed a god created the heaven and earth and everything in it but they didn't know his name. Isn't that fascinating? I was reminded of *Psalm 19* that says God's handiwork declares His glory – even to people who don't know His name.

Ladies Class was good today. It seemed like a ho-hum lesson. I can say that because I prepared this lesson series. But it turned out to be really good. God can use even ho-hum stuff!

It's that time of year again when...we get fresh ice every night. The snow and ice melt during the warm afternoons and then refreezes every night – to ensure maximum slickness!

Have a good week! 39 Days to furlough!

March 18, 2001

I got to teach several Bible lessons in Mongolian this week - Jesus Calming the Storm, the Sower and the Seed and the Sermon on the Mount. Great fun! My teacher told me that she thinks the story of Jesus being killed and coming back to life is a lie. OK. At least she is open and honest with me and still listening to my lessons.

I was walking along Monday afternoon and heard water trickling. I just stopped and enjoyed the sound because I hadn't heard that in a long time. Ice doesn't trickle.

Opened a window in our apartment for the first time since October when the windows were sealed for the winter. The air is crisp but feels wonderful!

Saturday I just stood and soaked up the sunshine. This week I downgraded from my full-length down coat to my leather jacket with lining. From mittens to leather gloves. From major boots to mid-weight boots. And I got rid of the long-handles on top. Yes, spring is definitely here!

We saw a parade Saturday honoring the military. Soldiers marched down the main street along with a little oompa band. We stopped and enjoyed it - just like country folks come to town. When they got to the Square, they did a little performing. Why does goose-stepping make chills go down my spine?

Excuse me! I'm not Russian!

I was walking along Saturday minding my own business. A woman about my age stepped toward me and hauled off and hit me on the arm. Really hard. Now I've been pushed, shoved, gouged, bumped into intentionally, and patted down by pickpockets and of course one time that kid slashed my pocket but this is the first time I have actually been hit. I guess she thought I was Russian. If I were Mongolian, I wouldn't like Russians either.

God speaks my language!

Being on the foreign field in a developing country causes lots of different emotions. I would like to tell you they are all wonderful. In fact, I could easily write so you would think that, but I have tried to be truthful in my writing. OK. I confess. I do not release the writing I do in my darkest hours because it is not fit for human consumption.

But the only way to describe this past week is - lonely. Yes, I have friends but either we struggle in their second language (English) or in my second language (Mongolian). Yes, I have dozens of email pals who stay in touch but that requires typing. I'm so tired of trying to have a phone conversation with drag so that what you say takes a few seconds to transmit. Or to be cut off in the middle of a conversation. I was doing instant messaging with the kids and my internet provider cut us off. I'm just tired of that. I look forward to having a real conversation - without interruptions - without struggling to find and pronounce the word I need.

Yes, I know I get to see everyone in just five weeks. It is ridiculous to be lonely at this point - after 18 months. No one ever said emotions were logical. Lots of people all around me yet I am lonely. Thankfully my God is always there - and He speaks my language.

> **It's that time of year again when...** walking is uncertain. In winter everything is solid ice so every step must be carefully placed. This time of year about 90% of the ice has melted so you are walking on dirt most of the time. Then without warning, you hit a patch of ice unexpectedly. You know to look for ice in shadows but sometimes even in the sun a particularly thick patch of ice will be hanging on.

32 Days! Love, Jenny

March 25, 2001
God's Definition of a Fool

This week at school I taught several Bible lessons including the story of the Wise Man and Foolish Man. At the end I asked "Are you like the wise man (hearing and following God's Word) or like the foolish man (hearing God's Word but not doing what it says)?"

When I taught that lesson to Amaglan, she was very quiet with a bad look on her face. I didn't see how my grammar and pronunciation could be that bad! She was quiet so long that finally I asked if my sentences were OK. She grumbled "yes" and then proceeded to argue with me about the lesson. Aw! Conviction evidences itself in many forms. She did not like what I said. She said I should not use the word "fool" because it is impolite. Mongolians do not want to be impolite in speaking although they will shove you and pick your pocket. Go figure! She wanted to substitute "lazy person" for the word "fool". I held my ground - or I should say - God's ground. I told her I wasn't saying this person was a fool. God said it.

After much discussion, she finally told me my lesson was good. (She was referring to the grammar and sentence structure.) I already knew it was good because it got through to her! Praise the Lord.

Counting the Days Until Furlough

Michael Jordan would be jealous!

Kids are the same all over the world! I went outside to take some pictures of teenage boys playing basketball. When they saw me taking pictures, you have never seen such moves and slam-dunks! Michael Jordan would be jealous!

I was taking a picture of a boy about eight years old. A girl came up behind him and held up two fingers behind his head. Some things are universal!

Don't keep me here against my will!

I have asked many of you to pray that there is no wind on the morning of April 20 - so our departure is not delayed. Now I have something else to add to that list. Several aimags in Mongolia have been quarantined because of foot and mouth disease. Three sections of Ulaanbaatar are quarantined. Soldiers are posted around the area and they will not allow any person or vehicle to go in or out. It is on our side of town - not too far from our apartment. Dennis heard the quarantine was for rabies and they were killing stray dogs. I heard it was foot and mouth disease. Whatever it is - I don't want to be trapped in this place.

I came willingly. I stayed willingly. I will return willingly after furlough. I just don't want to be trapped here against my will!!

It's that time of year again when...you have a choice of hat hair or windblown hair. Take your pick.

25 Days! Love from the windy side of the earth! Jenny

April 1, 2001
Oh! It's you Hal!

We were going across town to the baptizing service with 18 people crammed into a van designed for 12. We passed a policeman who blew his whistle. Our driver kept going. Passed a second policeman who blew his whistle. Our driver never flinched. One block later a policeman somehow convinced our driver that he better pull over.

Egi and the driver got out and talked to the policeman. We figured we were being stopped either for too many people in the van (ya think??? duh!!!) or because they were enforcing the new law forbidding microbuses on Peace Avenue.

After a few minutes, Egi and the driver come back, we pulled away and off we went. We asked Egi what happened. In his best English he said "When I told the policeman that Hal was in the van, he said to go right ahead. He apologized for not recognizing Hal as we zipped by."

Our friends in the van loved the humor! Then Egi got in really deep. He said "At first the policeman didn't remember who Hal was but then I told him - you know - his wife is Jenny. And then he let us go!"

We were too crowded to lift our feet but I think we needed to.

April 8, 2001

This morning I taught the ladies the story of Christ's death. I have never had more attentive students in my entire life! And they had really good questions. How blessed I am!

Only 12 More Days! 6 Mongolian Lessons. 1 Sunday. 1 or 2 snow storms!

Love, Jenny

April 15, 2001

Hope all of you had a wonderful Resurrection Day Celebration! We had precious services here in Ulaanbaatar. The Ladies Class was filled to capacity and I had the awesome privilege to teach about our risen Lord. I am sure I learned more than my students did. Even after all these years, I continue to find nuggets hidden in God's Word. Teaching here in Mongolia is like going on a walk with a child. You see things through their eyes and it is all fresh and new.

Sent Back to America with Love

We had 26 in church. I think that was the most we have ever had except for our special Christmas service. What a joy! I wasn't prepared for the overwhelming emotion I felt - knowing that this is our last Sunday here for three months. I tried to soak up the singing in Mongolian. And although we were sent from America with great love and affection and prayer, we are being sent back to America with an equal amount of love and affection and prayer. I will definitely miss these people. They are thieves! They have stolen our hearts!

Monday I will be teaching the story of the crucifixion to Amaglan. Then Tuesday Dennis and I are combining our language classes and will be watching the Jesus film in Mongolian. One of our teachers has never seen the film. The other one has seen it but has questions. Pray for us as we witness in this way.

Last Monday we had more snow than we have had since we arrived. It was beautiful! When there is a lot of snow, people carry their rugs (big room-size rugs) outside and put snow on them and them brush it off. They say it cleans them. Charlotte and I are not sure what kind of dirt they have. The kind we get on our rugs, needs more than a roll in the snow to come clean.

I did spring cleaning on Wednesday. Don't ask me why I felt a need to clean house before I leave for three months. I think it falls into that category of your mother telling you to change your underwear - in case you are in a car accident. You can just imagine the surgeon ready to do the procedure to save your life and the head nurse saying "Look at this kid's underwear! He didn't change this morning!" And the surgeon is so disgusted and distracted, you die before he regains his composure after seeing your dirty underwear.

Anyway, my house is cleaner now. And I feel better. Thank you Mom!

Thank you for your prayers that we have no wind on Friday so we can leave on time. Please continue to pray for us as we are on furlough. Furlough is not vacation. One look at our schedule proves that! We have much to get accomplished in a short time. We will be visiting over 40 churches in three months, plus all our doctor appointments, restocking of supplies, etc. We have time set aside for our kids and Mom and Dad. So much to do! We will be traveling thousands of miles. Please pray for our safety.

Signing off until August!
Love from the ends of the earth, Jenny

Furlough Happenings

I spent almost two years looking forward to furlough. It was wonderful, but what a shock to discover that I no longer belong there! I guess I thought I could feel at home here and there, but that's not the way it works. I am tempted to say that everyone and everything in America changed but I know in reality that I am the one who changed.

Furlough: What a fascinating, complex event. Long anticipated. Meticulously planned. Refreshing yet exhausting. Like a huge gulp of air before you go under water again. Familiar yet strange - all at the same time. Some moments (like time with our family) I wanted to last forever and other moments (like saying goodbye) I wanted to speed through because it hurt too much to linger. Here is a collage of precious memories and feelings I don't want to ever forget:

The thrill of that first glimpse of California poppies along the tarmac at the Los Angeles Airport The symbol of California - our homeland! Poppies along the highway. Poppies everywhere! Never noticed so many before. They never looked so beautiful before.

Hugs, hugs and more hugs. Strong, powerful "I have missed you" hugs.

Feeling like a fish out of water. America is our homeland but we feel like foreigners. We don't belong there.

Feeling like I just got off the boat. I probably looked that way too.

Worship in my mother tongue for the first time in two years - so strange.

So much stuff thrown away - heavy plastic forks at McDonald's, tissue and giftwrap, leftover food. Frivolous use of paper towels and plastic bags. Americans don't even wash and reuse plastic bags!

Counting the Days Until Furlough

The taste of that first hamburger...and the second...and the third.

The beauty of Coeur d'Alene Lake. Thank you Lord for a few days of rest.

Laughing and acting silly with old friends until we were doubled over and couldn't walk.

Stopping for a huckleberry milkshake after visiting a lake in the mountains of northern Idaho.

Precious hours with our children. Twelve hours squeezed in the car going to and from Southern California. Remembering family stories and jokes. Creating new family memories.

Screaming on rollercoasters. Thankful that although we are in our fifth decade, we can still go on rollercoasters with our kids!

The pride of attending Christopher's graduation and getting to hear in person about the early days at his first real job.

The pride of hearing Craig preach for the first time. He did an awesome job! I cried through the whole sermon but hey I used to cry when my kids did anything on stage - even if they were the daisy in the third row in the Kindergarten skit. My child was the very best daisy in the whole group and I was never prejudiced!

Countless hours and thousands of miles in the car going from church to church.

Renewing old acquaintances and making many new friends.

The joy of hearing of a precious soul saved in Mongolia.

Losing an hour at Long's Drugs - just walking up and down the aisles marveling at the variety of products.

Running through the hot, humid Little Rock Airport and almost missing our connecting flight.

Presenting the Mongolian work over and over and over again - and the Lord keeping it fresh every time.

The frustration of living out of a suitcase for weeks at a time.

Sleeping in dozens of different places - sometimes in the homes of strangers.

Trying to keep our act together - a real challenge.

Laying in Anne's hammock on the deck one afternoon with a cool breeze and a magazine and feeling terribly guilty for such decadence, but thank you Lord anyway.

Being in many churches - with beautiful buildings and loving people but not finding a single one where I would rather be than in Mongolia - where God has called us.

The thrill of catching myself thinking in Mongolian one day!!!

Wonderful pot bless dinners at churches. I have the additional pounds as proof!

Sitting by the campfire at a ladies retreat in Washington.

When AJ (age three) who was thoroughly enjoying playing with Papa Howie - asked "Why did Miss Jenny come?" He knew why Papa Howie had come to see him - to play with him. But Miss Jenny seemed to have no redeeming value!

The joy of seeing children growing into young adults.

The wonderful joy of seeing new faces at our sponsoring church - people saved in the last two years.

Drinking big tall glasses of cold milk - that tasted like milk should taste.

Cheerios and milk. Yum!

Quiet time with Mom and Dad. Sitting on the swing on the back patio watching the humming birds feed. Sitting in the front yard watching the birds in the birdbath and listening to the hymns being played on the church bells. Yes, there are still towns in America with that wonderful old tradition.

Thankful for our time in the States yet we are anxious to get back to work in the field of our calling. There is so much to do and so little time! What if this would be the year that Jesus comes?

Abundance

If you asked for a one-word description of America, it would be abundance. There is so much of everything! It was a shock to our system the first time we went to a grocery store on furlough. How many kinds of fruit juice does a person really need? Or cheese? Or cereal? We had difficulty taking it all in and making a decision. Our eyes felt tired from looking and our brain numb from the scope of options.

Things are good here in Mongolia compared to the early 1990's when people went hungry, but this country still cannot produce enough food to feed itself. Everything is imported and often those shipments consist of the products that did not sell in Western countries. You have to search for things and when you finally find it at the other end of town, there may be only a few available.

Oh but there is one area where abundance prevails. God's blessing! Oh how marvelously He is pouring out of His love and grace in this land! We are overwhelmed by that abundance! Each Sunday as people respond to God's Word, we wonder "Can there possibly be more? Can this continue?" Thank you, Lord for the privilege of living in this land of abundance!

Chapter Seventeen

THE HONEYMOON IS OVER

August 5, 2001

We arrived in Mongolia exactly two years ago today. I am so thankful to be where we are today instead of where we were two years ago. I wouldn't trade the last two years for anything but I wouldn't want to live through them again either!

When we first came to Mongolia, it was exciting, exotic and intriguing. The romance of starting a new life in a new culture was exhilarating. This time when we returned to Mongolia, we came out of love for the people because the romance is gone.

We know what the garbage smells like. We know how difficult the language is. We know how long the winters are and how difficult life is in a developing country. We know the loneliness, the frustration and the drudgery. But we also know God's abundant provision and the joy of seeing souls saved. So here we are back again - for another term.

We saw many changes in the three months we were out of the country. New buildings, new businesses, new faces. But we knew we were in Mongolia for sure. We were greeted by friends at the airport. Going down Peace Avenue, I saw a man urinating and not even bothering to turn his back to the street. Yep, that's Mongolia! The road was torn up...still. Driving down the street, dodging potholes and pedestrians felt like one of the roller coasters we rode at Disneyland - twisting, turning and jerking. But that's just driving in Ulaanbaatar!

Coming from the airport, I was in one car and Hal and Egi were in another car. No one in my car spoke much English so I was immediately thrown back into Mongolian while suffering from jet lag and after having not spoken it for three months. What a shock! They were full of questions and I was giving knee-jerk answers in Mongolian and then wondering if I said the right thing. I guess Mongolian is still buried somewhere deep in my subconscious. We have heard that after a full, complete break from the language, your second language skills develop rapidly. We pray that it is so!

Worship today was wonderful. It is so good to be back where we belong. Once again we see so much that needs to be done for the Lord. There are so many who need to hear about Christ. I wish there were 72 hours in every day and 20 months in every year.

It's that time of year again when....it is hot during the day but every evening it cools down with a wonderful breeze blowing in off the steppe.

August 12, 2001

It's been hot this week. Not as hot as Fresno in June. Not as hot as Arkansas in July. But hot for Mongolia. This morning I woke to the glorious sound of rain slowly dripping on metal. Beautiful, drizzly, drippy, refreshing rain! Blessed relief from the heat! And a wonderful cool breeze coming through the window. This means the grass will grow and the animals will have feed and the people won't starve.

We walked to church in the rain and then sat through services with that wonderful breeze coming through the window. Precious memories!

We are now officially settled. Got the two years' supply of things tucked away and the apartment in decent order. Took longer than I expected but that's OK. We ate horshols this week. They were delicious!

I guess our furlough "took". Hal and I ran into the school principal the other day. She said our faces looked refreshed. She should know.

Mongolia is definitely changing. This week I bought a prepaid international long distance phone card. Supposed to work just like prepaid phone cards in the States. Did you catch that "supposed to" in there? It doesn't recognize my account number. I have to walk back to the phone office next week. This is normal. If I get it to work in less than three trips, I'll be truly blessed.

Escalator Down

Ulaanbaatar has the country's first (and only) escalator. One floor. Up only. If "escalate" means to go up and if you take the "Escalator Down", do you stay in the same place? Like debits and credits cancelling each other out? Inquiring minds want to know!

The escalator was put in a new Korean market that looks very much like a Walmart. Not exactly the same range of products - but a nice selection. And they have baskets you push and cash registers. What excited me most is they have pasteurized milk that tastes good!! Not like Mongolian milk that tastes like a barnyard smells. Even though it is very expensive, I'm so thankful to have it. Hope the store doesn't go out of business in a few months. (Afternote: It didn't go out of business but they quit carrying the milk I liked.)

Christianity is under attack here. Recently a young man died at a church worksite from an accident. The parents (who are Buddhist) said if their son had not been a Christian, he would not have been working there and he would not have died. And if the country had not become a democracy, Christianity would not have been here. Please pray for those who oppose Christianity in this country.

Horse's Hooves

On Saturday I was working in the kitchen and suddenly I heard a sound that made me go to the window and look out. Every time I hear that sound, I go to the window. I know exactly what I am going to see, yet I go. Every time!

The sound is the wonderful, rhythmic klip klop, klip klop of a horse's hooves on the street below. What I always see is a single horse pulling an old cart laden with stuff. The cart seems to set at an angle with the tongue sloping upward so that as the horse trots along, the cart bounces rhythmically.

I absolutely love the sound of horse hooves on blacktop! But it also makes me sad because I see all the changes happening in Ulaanbaatar and I know that very soon, I will no longer hear that sound. It happened in America. The horses and carriages that once transported Americans everywhere were replaced by the automobile. It didn't change instantly from carriage ruts to four-lane freeways. It happened gradually. I doubt anyone even took note of the final time horse's hooves were heard on the street in America. But there was a last time.

God has given me the awesome privilege of living in a place where that sound is still around. Well.....not downtown Ulaanbaatar anymore. There just isn't enough room. But here on the Eastern edges of town, the horse carts are still used to deliver goods purchased at the open-air market. But we are getting more and more cars. In addition to the traffic jams and air pollution, it means someday the disappearance of horsedrawn carts. And that makes me sad.

Who am I to deprive these people of progress. (I suppose a car is better than a horse.) But the most important thing democracy has brought to Mongolia is the gospel.

I began my language review this past week. We have made far more progress in the Mongolian language than we think. This past week, we went to visit a church member thinking that his daughter (who is one of our translators) would be there. But the daughter wasn't there. So Hal and I visited for over an hour - all in Mongolian. That's progress! Praise the Lord!

> **It's that time of year again when...** The calendar says summer but the weather says autumn....so I reach for a jacket.

We had a first at church this morning. Biaraa who became a Christian last summer and who now leads worship at church, prayed publicly for the first time. Now that is not a big deal to some people but it was a big step for Biaraa. Oh how I rejoiced as I listened to this young Christian express praise and adoration to God! I know he used simple sentences because I understood them!!!

God loves a simple prayer from the heart more than all the flowery religious jargon from the lips only! We as earthly parents know what a joy it is when our children express their love to us. Even if the words are not perfectly formed and the child only uses short, easy words. Yet that expression from the heart is so special. I believe God smiled this morning. I know I did - through tears of rejoicing.

Still glad to be called to this place. Love, Jenny

August 26, 2001
Phone booths outdated. No problem in Mongolia.

I heard a newsclip on CNN this week. It said that pay phones in America may be going the way of the buggy whip. There is simply not much market for pay phones since almost everyone has a cell phone. So pay phones are being removed except in the most profitable locations.

Mongolia may actually be ahead of the game here. We have never had phone booths. We do have pay phones though. People sit on the street with a little metal stand/table and a phone. Sometimes they string the phone cord from a nearby building. Sometimes people walk around the Square in the middle of town with hand phones. You make your call and pay them. So when pay phones go out of style, it will be a simple thing here in Ulaanbaatar.

Recently I was bemoaning that horse carts were disappearing here in Ulaanbaatar. This week on the road behind our apartment, two cowboys herded a group of horses (maybe eight or ten) right down the road. OK, so maybe things aren't changing that fast.

> **It's that time of year when....** Every afternoon I enjoy hearing the clicking of the old men's domino game on the table below our window.

September 9, 2001

Found out this week that I know the books of the New Testament in Mongolian - backwards! Naara now does the drills on Wednesday nights to learn the books of the New Testament. Our drill this week was to say them backwards. I wasn't even sure I could say them in English backwards, but I did - in Mongolian! Maybe there is hope.

We had real Mongolian BBQ this week. No, it is not like the franchise in America called Mongolian BBQ - which we think originated in Inner Mongolia which is part of China.

On Friday we went to pick potatoes at Egi's potato patch. We hope he keeps his day job because a farmer, he ain't. The potatoes were very small - some the size of a large bean. He planted them too late so his growing season was even shorter than the Mongolian growing season - which is already short!

Afterwards, we had horhok - Mongolian BBQ. They built a small campfire beside the river. They took rocks out of the river and put them in the fire until they got hot. Then they had brought a metal pot shaped like a large wok. Into it they put hunks of mutton, the hot rocks, potatoes (freshly dug and washed in the river), carrot, onion, turnip, salt and a little water. They had a wooden lid thing. After about an hour, we ate. It was delicious! The broth was wonderful too. We sat near the fire, in the brisk breeze and ate this delicious Mongolian picnic.

David and Alice arrived to minister while Dennis and Charlotte are gone. We had a share time on Sunday and the Mongolians gave their testimonies. Wow! What a blessing! We heard one man say "My life is difficult. Some of my old friends say I am crazy. But my heart is full. I am happy since I became a Christian."

Still good to be here at the ends of the earth, Jenny

September 16, 2001
God is still in control.

What a tragic week for the world! We have had continuous TV coverage since the first attack. What a sickening, helpless feeling to watch your homeland under attack wondering which city will be the next target. I am so thankful we have the confidence that God is still in control although it seems the whole world is out of control. The perpetrators intended this for evil, but I pray that God will make something good of it. I pray that God gives our leaders wisdom during the next few weeks and months as extremely important decisions are made.

So proud to be an American! What a thrill to see so many flags being flown in America. One of my favorite sights here in Mongolia is the US Embassy. The Russian Embassy is larger. The Japanese Embassy is newer. The Turkish Embassy is more impressive. The Chinese Embassy is located in a better section of town. The US Embassy is actually quite utilitarian and ugly but it has that most resplendent of all fabrics - the Stars and Stripes - high on a flag pole, wafting in the Mongolian wind. My homeland - far from perfect - far from Godly - yet the land that I love.

(God) stand beside her and guide her through the night with the light from above.

Some have asked how this event is being viewed outside the United States. I can only speak for my little corner of the world. We have had Mongolian friends and acquaintances call us - just to see if our family is safe and to express their condolences for America. I have not heard a single negative word toward America through all of this. This baby democracy is watching to see how the largest of all democracies is handling difficult times. The people here have never seen America at its most patriotic. Indeed my generation has only seen pictures of such patriotism during WWII. All we have ever known is the division and confusion of the Vietnam Era.

I love the patriotism I see although I am sorry it took such a horrible tragedy to prompt it. I am the one who tears up every single time I hear the National Anthem at a football game. Hal is the one who trained our boys at a very young age, the proper respect to be shown during the National Anthem and displaying of the flag. And he even expected that behavior during their cool teen years when such old-fashioned traditions stood out like a sore thumb. Yes, we are diehard patriots. People in a foreign land are called expatriates, but there is not a lot of "ex" in our hearts right now.

May this week be far less dramatic than last week.
Love, Jenny

Because He Lives

Every week has a defining moment - one that stands out above all the other moments. This morning in church as we were singing, God's goodness just swept over my soul so that my worship came from my heart! We were singing "Because He Lives" in Mongolian. The words don't rhyme in this language. There is not a steady, even beat. In fact, you often have to push to get all the syllables in. But you will never hear a sweeter sound in all the world than Mongolians who face extreme difficulties everyday but they now know Christ as Savior and life-giver and they raise their voices to sing.

> Because He lives, I can face tomorrow.
> Because He lives, all fear is gone.
> Because I know who holds tomorrow.
> And life is worth the living just because He lives!

Oh what a privilege to be here to share the Tomorrow Holder with these precious people!

Please help Jenny!

A precious moment. Dogi cleans my house on Fridays before going to class in the afternoon. As I prepared our lunch, I was telling her about how hard it is to translate the children's material into Mongolian. It is taking me far longer than I expected.

After we sat down to eat, I asked her to offer thanks for the food. Of course, she prayed in Mongolian. She asked God to help me learn Mongolian and help me to translate the material for the children. Can you imagine how precious that is to me? And the best part - I understood her Mongolian!!! I believe God has heard my hundreds of requests to speak the language but now He is getting the request in Mongolian too. That kinda wipes out any discouragement that I was feeling.

God provides before we know we have a need!

As we returned from furlough, my aunt gave us some money and told us to use it for anything we wanted. Hal and I thought of a couple different things, but nothing really grabbed us. So we tucked the money away. God had a plan for that money!

Our largest room at church had been being filled to capacity every Sunday. We asked the landlady if we could knock out a wall and she said no. She offered to rent us the large basement room, but the rent was ridiculously high so Hal told her no. For a month we continued to look for another space and we prayed.

Then the landlord came to Hal offering the space for half the earlier quoted amount but we had to pay half the cost of remodeling it. Guess how much our half was? Almost exactly the amount of money my aunt gave us! God always provides what we need when we need it....or a few months before!

October 7, 2001

Do you ever wonder why God is so good to us? I'm doing that today. We had 31 people in worship services this morning. The room was crammed! I sat in front with my knees touching the front of the pulpit. Why does God bless us with so many opportunities? I don't understand it. He blesses in spite of our faults and weaknesses.

I had a "fall down" kind of week. First I fell on the way to Bible Study Wednesday night. I didn't see a rock sticking up out of the ground. Hal grabbed me and broke my fall a little but I still bruised my elbow and knee.

Thou hast enlarged my steps under me, that my feet did not slip.
Psalm 18:36

Saturday we went out to Terelj Park with our neighbors and David and Alice. We stopped along the way because there was a yak - saddled and available for riding. Hal rode it. Bilgoon rode it. I tried. Ended up on my backside. (I don't think the yak liked women.) Thankfully I barely missed a big rock (that could have done some serious damage). I also missed a big pile of yak poop (that could have made a big mess).

Borrowing and Lending

There are aspects of this culture that continue to amaze us. One thing we have learned is that the Mongolian view of borrowing and lending is different from ours.

Now, first you should know that I was raised with the notion that you don't borrow except as a last resort. If you are absolutely in a bind, you cannot live without an item and there is no other way to get it, then and only then, do you consider borrowing as an option. And of course, you repay it immediately with a little extra as thanks.

Here in Mongolia borrowing is a way of life. They borrow all the time. Furthermore, the mindset is that if you have something and I ask for it, you are obligated to give it to me. If I have money and you ask to borrow it, I must lend it even if the money is set aside for the rent next week.

This week I learned the ultimate of this mindset. My teacher is the middle of three girls. When she was two years old, their neighbors' two children died. They wanted children very much but could not have any more so they asked their neighbors (my teacher's parents) if they could adopt one of their children.

My teacher's mother felt she could not give up one of her children. But the father's logic was as follows: "We are blessed with three healthy children. Our neighbors have none. They are good people. They want one of our children, we must give them one." Seriously!! And that's what they did! My teacher was loaned to the neighbor. They adopted her but she kept her father's name. She was raised knowing her birth parents were the neighbors and the ones raising her were her adopted parents. She said her father always told her he loved her the most of all his children. But she could never understand why he gave her away if he loved her the most.

The Honeymoon is Over

Now there is a cultural mindset for you!

A Human Shield

Twice a week I travel by bus across town to class. The bus is always "packed, jammed, squished, can't get another person on board" crowded. Sometimes I have to wait for a second bus because no one else can physically get on board. Sometimes the driver will take off with the door open and people hanging out the door. (Sorta like riding the cable cars in San Francisco.)

One day recently I was pushing to get onto the bus. The young man behind me was gently pushing my back so that the front of my body was forcing people out of the way. (A human shield???) Of course, he was doing this because he wanted on also. But the wall of humanity would not give.

The toll-taker was standing on the step. He was a strong young man. He reached down and put his arm around the back of my waist and between his pulling and the other young man's pushing, my body forced the wall of people back enough for us to get on. There was no pole that I could reach but there was no way I was going to fall down. I think if the bus had turned over, we would have remained wedged together. Through all of this I kept my arm across my bag to discourage pickpockets.

So that is what I deal with two mornings a week. As I stand crammed in like a human sardine, I pray that heaven will be just that crowded! And I realize that it is likely that many of the people around me are not Christians. And in case I have forgotten exactly why I am doing all of this, I am then reminded. I am learning to speak Mongolian in order to tell souls about Christ. That is what it is all about.

October 21, 2001
Words Fail Me

Incredible! Awesome! Mind-boggling! Indescribable! Overwhelming! Wow! Wonderful! Motivating! Rejuvenating! Blessed! Words cannot describe our feelings today. Friendship Day at Rich

Heart Baptist Church was beyond words! My cup overflowed this morning...and so did my eyes!

The basement room didn't get finished but we used it anyway. The floor was dirty rough cement. The walls needed paint. The window frames were bare wood. We had no electricity. But those things are hardly worth mentioning. They faded into nothingness. We were blessed with 82 people in attendance - a new record attendance. We served tea and pastry and had a wonderful time of fellowship. The singing was great. David preached the Word and many people heard about the best friend of all - Jesus.

God is so awesome! His plans are so much bigger than our plans. How many times do we limit Him because of our tiny, human ideas and plans? God forgive us. Expand our vision. Lengthen our days. Increase our strength. Help our unbelief.

An awesome week at the ends of the earth!

So glad to be here. Love, Jenny

November 4, 2001
What is God preparing you for?

Well, winter has finally arrived. It snowed all day yesterday. Ulaanbaatar is sporting a beautiful new coat. It is cold but refreshing. Not the hard, painful cold that we get from December to February.

Nothing real dramatic this week. Just a normal week serving the Lord. This morning I was reminded of something. God started preparing me for this work many decades ago. In fact He has been preparing me for this work all of my life and I am so thankful for that.

I began to teach children's Sunday School as soon as I graduated from high school. I taught the four year old boys. Mary was the department head and my mentor. She had taught children for many years. She taught me many things about sharing the beautiful Bible stories with little ones. But she taught me something even more important - to love the children.

Mary is a beautiful lady - always immaculately well-dressed with very nice clothes, jewelry and hair. Yet I saw her pick up children who were dirty and put them on her lap to hug them. She seemed to never once think about her nice dress or be concerned that the child was dirty - yet knowing Mary as I do, she did not like the dirt. That is God's love in action - not human love.

This morning at the end of services a little girl ran to me with a big smile on her face. I picked her up and she gave me a big long hug. She was not exactly clean and she smelled like mutton. A smell like no other. Musty. Earthy. Dirty. Not pleasant to the non-Mongolian nose. As I hugged this precious little girl who stunk, a picture of Mary holding a dirty little child flashed through my mind. And I thanked God for all the preparation He has invested in me.

November 18, 2001
"Leaving the Country" Sale

I never cared for garage sales in America. I had no desire to go through other people's junk. I certainly never expected to find anything I would have. But in a place like Mongolia, there is one kind of sale you definitely want to attend. When a long-term missionary is leaving the field - now there is a sale to tickle the fancy of remaining missionaries! You can find all the goodies from the States - that you can't find here in Mongolia. Spices, Christmas things, Christian books, craft items, kitchen utensils.

We just returned from furlough and from the amount of stuff we brought back, you would think we could not possibly need or want another thing for years, if ever. But....Saturday our neighbors who are from Canada and have been here ten years - had a sale. They are leaving the country and selling everything.

I found little things like a pastry blender, big bags of chocolate chips, a glass measuring cup. And the really big thing - a complete set of flannelgraph - Old and New Testament - already cut out and with all the backgrounds. One time my friend Elaine and I cut out such a set. I never wanted to see another pair of scissors as long as I lived! I thought my hand would never be the same! And this set is already cut out for me. My neighbor was so happy that the set was going to someone who will use it. You think it is an accident that this item became available just a couple months before we start teaching children? No way!

Changing of the Guard

Within the last year we have personally known of four long-term missionaries leaving Mongolia. It is almost like a changing of the guard. I don't begrudge them. They served the first shift and we are serving the second. There is still so much to do here. I don't know why God moves people to new fields, but I don't question. Someday we will be the ones conducting the sale. But as I see them leave, I have no desire to leave. I feel honored to remain here. Excited to do this work.

But the one thing I want from departing missionaries that they cannot give me - their Mongolian fluency. How wonderful it would be if they could download their language skills and I could upload them. That's not the way it works though!

God's provision is never depleted.

This week my teacher asked me to talk about Christmas - using Mongolian, of course. I explained that so much of what they see about Christmas (trees, tinsel, Santa, reindeer, etc.) is American culture. It has nothing to do with the real reason for Christmas - the birth of the Messiah. She asked about the giving of gifts. I told her about the wise men coming from the East (I think they might have been Mongolian) to present gifts to the Christ child. And now we give gifts at Christmastime.

Then she asked a very interesting question. "Do American stores run out of gifts before Christmas?" I had to smile as I thought of the mountains of goods in the stores - both the day before Christmas and the day after (on sale, of course). I told her "No. The stores do not run out of gifts." You see, Mongolian stores regularly run out of things. You can never count on any given product on any given day.

It made me think - how blessed we are in America. We have unlimited provision. But even more important - I am blessed because I have God's unlimited provision. It is never depleted - never! And that is the message we came to deliver to these precious people who have been deprived of the knowledge of God's grace for so many decades.

So many need to hear. So many need to accept. So much to do. So little time.

December 2, 2001
Dunking To Be Done

This morning after the message, Hal gave the usual invitation for people to come forward to be saved or to request baptism. We were aware of four or five people who wanted to be baptized. But 13 people came forward!!! We couldn't believe our eyes.

Incredible! Amazing! Awesome! Unbelievable! Why am I so shocked when I have been praying for every single person who went forward? When I pray, I truly do believe God will answer but then when He does, it is so overwhelming!

So Dennis has got some dunkin' to do when he returns. Hal says he is going to be in the water so long, he will look like a prune. We know he will love it. Dennis and Charlotte are in the air right now traveling back so this will be their welcome home surprise. And boy will they be pleased! What a mighty God we serve!

God is certainly rearranging my written prayer list! I don't rewrite it very often because I love to see all those earlier prayer requests marked off with a PTL (Praise the Lord) beside each one! It increases my faith for the remaining names on the list!

The wedding was beautiful. We had really precious time with our children. Stephanie fixed a delicious Thanksgiving dinner. We just enjoyed doing ordinary things with our children. I feel so blessed. Most people have to have a brush with death before they appreciate how precious time is. But all I had to do was go on the foreign mission field and I have learned to savor such moments.

Going and coming was easier this time because we weren't gone long enough to experience any cultural adjustment coming back in. And since we had just been in the States, even the excess of Christmas didn't shock us too much. But one aspect of this thing will never get easy - saying goodbye. I consider myself somewhat of an expert on this topic.

Which part of goodbye is good?

In Mongolian the word for goodbye is biartie. It means "with joy". Exactly what is good about saying goodbye? I can't find anything good about it. If by chance my leaving someone makes me joyful or feel good, I am likely to not even say anything. And when we leave people we love - we say "with joy" or "good". I don't think so!

I don't know why I complain. It was such a special blessing to get to see my kids again. And we weren't saying goodbye beside a hospital bed, or at a graveside or at prison gates. Hal and I are returning to a work we really love. We are leaving kids who love the Lord and are productive citizens. All of us are healthy and happy - except when we say goodbye. So I guess I really should be doing this with joy. I always survive these times but it will never get easy. Never!

December 9, 2001

Have you ever been tired in a good way? That's what I am tonight.

We had a good lesson at ladies meeting on Saturday. I had brought little candles, greenery and Christmas ribbon from the States. You should have seen how happy they were with that little snippet of a craft! It sure doesn't take much to make them happy.

Then Saturday afternoon was class for people wanting to be baptized. What a joy to listen to the people tell how they came to know Christ. Saturday night I prepared food for Sunday.

Sunday we had Sunday School, church, dinner and fellowship, more testimonies and then we went across town for the baptism service. Egi had arranged for a bus to take us, but after ten minutes, it had not come. So he hijacked another bus. That's a fact! Somehow he managed to convince a private bus to stop, make their passengers get off and then pick us up. It was filled to overflowing and Egi and Hal had to take a taxi.

Ten people were baptized! Wow! What a joy! We have four more people who will be baptized in January! One is a lady in her 70's whose husband became a Christian last June. Which proves that God can work on hearts of any age!

It feels so good to be tired from doing God's work.

Have a good week! Jenny

December 16, 2001

God is so good! I was sitting in church this morning listening to the beautiful hymns in Mongolian and rehearsing in my mind how awesome our God is! My heart was full and of course, my eyes overflowed. I am so privileged to be here! Why did God pick us to come to Mongolia? Hal and I are very unlikely candidates to be missionaries. You can ask anyone and they will tell you. We don't fit any profile you would expect. Even now, we don't behave like normal missionaries yet God allows us to have a small part in His work. I don't think I will ever understand why but that does not prevent me from being thankful that God called and we answered.

Then.......at the end of service 11 people came forward! One accepted Christ as Savior. All the others professed having accepted Christ and wanted to be baptized and join our church. It is absolutely incredible! Ten were baptized last Sunday. Five others came forward last week. Then another 11 today! It boggles my mind! Is it an accident that this is happening now - after two long years in this country? After we have completed furlough? Just now as our visas allow us more time to minister? Accident? Coincidence? Nope. I don't believe in happenstance. God directs in all things. It's just sometimes we see it more clearly than other times.

Scattering Precious Seed

Some things in this country are really hard - mostly physical things. Some things are extremely easy - especially spiritual things.

We had a leak in a radiator this week. A common occurrence unfortunately. We called the landlady who came with the plumber. He examined it and then we were all waiting for a second plumber -

the one who carries the horsehair with which they "fix" (I use that term loosely!) literally everything!

Anyway, the plumber saw a Bible on the desk. He and I began to talk. (What a joy that I can do that!) He said he was a believer but he doesn't attend church. My landlady was standing there and said "Jenny's church is nearby". Now, you have to realize my landlady is Buddhist - going to temple and giving the lama money (her words). One time Dema was here and witnessed to her and the landlady called Dema a fool for following a Western God.

Anyway, I gave the plumber a map to our church and explained the times of our services. The landlady then began to say that Buddhism and Christianity are the same. I pretended I did not understand - to buy some time to digest it and formulate my answer in Mongolian. She repeated it slowly and deliberately. I could no longer feign ignorance so I told her no - there are many differences. The plumber backed me up with lots of full-speed Mongolian that I didn't catch. But I think he was witnessing to her!

Then the plumber asked if he could have a Bible that we had laying there. I said yes and gave him one. Then the landlady asked if she could have one!!!! Imagine my surprise since she felt Christianity was foolish! I'm standing there thinking - this is too easy! So now my Buddhist believing, temple-going landlady is carrying a portion of God's Word. The living word of God - which will not return void.

Let's Play Like

When I was a little girl, I would play house out under the trees. I would use cans, boards, rocks - anything available and "play like" it was other stuff. "Let's play like this is a sofa. Let's play like this is a wall and play like this is a stove."

This morning Charlotte and I arrived at church with our food. We both had sandwiches that contained mayonnaise. For some reason our church building is hot inside this year. (I'm not complaining.) We have no refrigerator and we were concerned about our sandwiches spoiling. So we began to search for a solution.

We have a small deck, but if we put our food outside it would freeze. So we put our food between the double doors going out on the deck. The ice on the inside of the outside door was a perfect cool place. We used dish towels, canvas bags and the curtain to build an enclosure to contain the cool air. Then we looked at each other and said "let's play like this is a refrigerator!" That's what brought on the walk down memory lane as noted above.

We do a lot of "play liking" here. But we don't have to "play like" we are being blessed by God. That is genuine!

January 13. 2002
Missionary is in and out of prison!

No, I didn't have a brush with the law. I began computer classes for the staff of the youth prison. Very interesting. The armed guards don't bother me. Hey! I've traveled through American airports since September 11 so I'm accustomed to that!

I must do the training with the employees at their desk while they do their jobs. One guy isn't too busy so that's not a problem. The other lady is the receptionist for all visitors to the prison. It is a real challenge to teach in the midst of that but I have no choice. The first day we got interrupted about ten times in one hour. At each of these desks there is also a second person learning computers.

The computers they have are 486's. Oh my goodness! I forgot how slow those old computers are! You could knit a sweater while it opens Word! And the receptionist uses an old dot matrix printer. I haven't touched one of those in years! I had forgotten that ripping sound it makes as it prints. And when she prepares a letter, she uses carbon paper because they do not have a copier. I haven't seen carbon paper is decades!

Interesting how God prepared me for his assignment. About three years before we came to Mongolia, my job at the law firm changed and I became the systems administrator in addition to everything else I did. I confess I was not terribly happy about crawling around under desks to work on computers and doing that techie stuff - including training. But little did I know, God was just getting me ready for Mongolia.

It is fun to teach people and see the light bulbs go on in their eyes. One employee at the prison worked on a manual typewriter (where you reach with your left hand and move the carriage to the next line) until they put her on a computer - with no instruction. I have seen people use computers like big typewriters before, but bless her heart, this lady really does that!

She only knew how to hit the letter keys, space key and backspace key. She didn't know that if you hit the Enter key you go to the next line. So when she got to the end of a line and wanted to go to the next line, she hit the space bar a gazillion times which took her waaaaay out to the right edge of the line and finally back to the next line. She didn't even know you could hold down the space bar and get repeated spaces so she inserted the spaces one at a time! This week when I showed her how to get a new line to type on, she just grinned. You can imagine the thrill when I showed her how to center a line with one keystroke. And copying and pasting is beyond anything she ever imagined!

I helped her format a letter she was doing. I asked if she wanted to save it. She said "no". I asked what she would do if she found a typo or if her boss changed his mind about something in the letter. She said she would retype it!!! I just moaned. Then we discussed saving documents.

We came here for the purpose of teaching these people how Christ will save their souls (by the way, a lady gave her heart to the Lord Sunday morning after church. PTL!) not about saving documents, but it is one of the ways we get to stay here. So it's nice that it gives me satisfaction to make life just a little easier for these precious people who know about as much about efficiency and automation as they do about God.

So I teach computers …in order to get a visa to live here …in order to share the gospel. What a deal!

Still glad to be here! Jenny

Chapter Eighteen

SCENES I CANNOT FORGET

Though these scenes have faded from my sight, my heart cannot forget....

Loved Despite our Sin

At first glance I presumed the young man on the bus was a drunk. I kept my bag close to my body. I noticed he was very dirty – like he lived on the street. He was probably in his late 20's. Then I noticed that he was with a young woman. I never got a good look at her face. I did notice her hands - dirt caked around the nails and knuckles that had not seen soap in many days.

They were both bundled up in dirty coats and scarves that cold January morning. The man's outer coat had been an expensive garment at one time. I recognized the stylish lines despite the wear and tear. The rips had been carefully mended – with thread that did not match, but the stitches were neat and well-placed. The man had a backpack that had the straps sewn back on – with the same sturdy white thread. The backpack had been slashed a few times and those rips had been repaired also. The zipper was ruined so it too was sewn together but in long, loose stitches that could be easily removed.

The girl got a seat. Because I was still standing I could see what they were doing. She had a dingy white rice bag with food inside. It looked like hard white cheese or hard pastry. She reached in with her dirty hand and carefully broke off a small piece and ate it. The man removed his filthy mitten and got himself a small piece to eat also. He leaned down near the girl when he ate – like he was embarrassed to be eating in public.

I then realized that he didn't have the look of a pickpocket. Thieves have a certain look in their eyes. I have learned to identify that look. He didn't have it.

Then the seat in front of the woman became available so the man sat down but he turned to face the girl so I could see him clearly. It was then that I really looked at his face. He was no drunk. His eyes were as clear as mine. His complexion was clear though smudged with dirt. He looked at the girl and then he tenderly brushed a hair or eyelash off her cheek. His eyes were speaking volumes. They were gentle. He loved that girl. Not a sensuous, come-on type of love. He really cared for her. But his eyes were sad too – probably because of their circumstances. I could only imagine that he was thinking how beautiful she was – despite the dirt.

My guess is they had come into the city from the countryside to try and make a living during the hard winter. I'm certain they had slept in the sewer or some empty shed the night before. They were probably riding the bus to get warm and were eating their breakfast on the bus so their hands didn't freeze. I don't even want to think about where they got the scraps of food.

I can't forget the look in his eyes. He loved her despite her appearance. Like Jesus loves us despite the filthiness of our sins.

> *But God commendeth his love toward us, in that,*
> *while we were yet sinners, Christ died for us.*
> *Romans 5:8*

Hopelessness

We sat in the living room of the bereaved family. The mother had just passed away. Her body lay in the other room – awaiting burial in a few days. All shiny objects (mirrors, television, etc.) were covered with cloth. Incense was burning at the shrine for the deceased. The room was filled with people of all ages. All were grief-stricken. The faces showed the marked signs of total despair with no hope beyond this life. They know this life will end – as it does for everyone. Then what? There were two Christians among the mourners. They were hurting too but it was different. They have a hope that only comes in knowing Christ as savior.

The look of hopelessness – I can't forget it.

For thou art my hope, O Lord God: thou art my trust...
Psalm 71:5

God changes lives.

We sat in the living room having prayer with a Mongolian pastor – a young man who as a teenager was the head of the largest gang in a city near the Russian border. Now that leadership ability is channeled for the cause of Christ and he is the pastor of the largest church in the city he once terrorized. He has a vision and a burning desire to see his country won for Christ. His prayer came from his heart with a sincerity and burden that cannot be faked. He prayed "God please bring the complete Bible to my country. We have waited so long! I want to see Mongolians saved."

What is truth?

It was a Saturday afternoon – bright, sunny, very cold. It was snowing lightly outside. The one-room house in which we sat was unbelievably warm from the wood stove. We had eaten a meal of Mongolian food – buuz, horshol, pastry, milk tea. The 70 year-old man said he had some questions for Dennis.

What is truth he asked? Dennis began to share the way, the truth and the life. One sentence at a time was slowly translated for him. As I sat beside Dennis on the bed (used as a couch during the day), I silently prayed for God to give him just the right words, for the translation to be clear and for the man to understand.

Then I noticed the others. The daughter was listening carefully. The mother was attentive. Such a sweet lady – who needs salvation

– just like the father. And the aunt who was crippled from a stroke. She listened carefully also. You could hear a pin drop except for the sound of the gospel being proclaimed – first in English, then in Mongolian.

Just a few short weeks later the aunt had another stroke. We never know when we are presenting the gospel to someone for the very last time. Oh that we always present it with urgency as if the person is about to die and slip into hell – because they might be!

The aunt – with crippled arm – listening to the gospel. The father asking profound questions. The mother listening carefully for the answers to her husband's questions. A scene I will never forget.

Afternote: The aunt recovered from the stroke and testified that she had accepted Christ as savior before her stroke. The father was saved and baptized in the spring of 2001. The mother was saved and baptized later that same year. Truly amazing that two people in their 70's made the life-changing decision to confess their sins and invite Christ into their lives!

Just Praying

As we were waiting for church to begin, guitar music was being played softly. I looked up and there was a young Mongolian man on the front row with his head in his hands praying for the service. I wish you could have seen him. It would have touched your heart.

No one ever told me about Jesus before.

The cool evening breeze was the perfect ending for a glorious day. White puffy clouds accented the green mountains and brilliant blue sky. Although it was early evening, the summer sun remained high in the sky. The sheep, goats and yak were off grazing somewhere. A perfect time to lean against the ger and rest a bit.

"Has anyone ever told you about Jesus?" The brown-skinned man with the toothless smile thought about that question and finally answered "No. I don't know who he is." And so the missionary began to explain that Jesus is the Son of God. The missionary told how the Lord of the Universe who created the world and all that is in it wanted a relationship with man, but man chose to sin and that relationship was broken. With a diagram drawn in the dirt with a stick, the man heard how God provided a way to restore the breach between God and man - the way, truth and life - Jesus!

The man's face could not hide the amazement at the incredible story he was hearing for the very first time! I will never forget the look on his face!

When asked about life after death, the man said he thought if you did good things, you went to a better life. If you did bad things, you returned as a lower life form. Very typical Buddhist thinking. Then Dennis explained that no amount of good works can qualify you for heaven. Only by believing in Jesus, God's Son, will we ever see the beauty and majesty of heaven.

The man agreed to think about the things he had been told and to read the gospel of John we gave him. Pray for MoonkJargal and his family – far away from any church but never away from God's presence. Please pray that we missionaries will never lose sight of the reason we are here. It is simple. We came to share the gospel with a people who have never heard! *Ye shall be witnesses unto me...unto the uttermost part of the earth. Acts 1:8*

Oh what a difference since Jesus passed by!

All over Mongolia, you see ovoos – a pile of rocks with a stick in the middle decorated with blue cloth. As Mongolians drive across the countryside, they stop at each ovoo, walk around it three times for good luck and then drink vodka. We have heard that sometimes drivers are completely drunk by the end of the day – from stopping at ovoos.

We were going to the countryside for a few days. The section of road we were traveling happened to be fairly decent and we were scooting along when suddenly Biaraa slammed on the brakes without warning. He pulled off the road just beyond an ovoo. All of us were confused, but he explained. "Before I was a Christian, I stopped at ovoos and drank vodka. Now I am saved. I want to stop and pray." Then he asked his daughter to pray before we took a short break to stretch our legs.

I don't know if you believe we can laugh while we pray, but all of us were doing just that! We couldn't keep from laughing because of the joy to see how God can change the life of a man! To God be the glory for the things He has done!

Therefore if any man be in Christ, he is a new creature: old things are passed away; behold, all things are become new.
II Corinthians 5:17

She looked into my heart!

I went to the home of my language helper several times a week to practice Mongolian. She had been hit and dragged by a large truck. She lost her right leg and had injuries to her other leg, both arms and a head injury (causing her to be in a coma for a couple of weeks). She is Buddhist – the daughter of a Buddhist lama. Dema has witnessed to her for years of the wonderful change that comes with knowing Christ as savior.

Once I had the privilege of sharing the gospel with her with Dema translating. Many other times I sat alone with her in her living room, within arm's reach of her Buddhist shrine – complete with food offerings – and I shared with her (in my best Mongolian) that God loves her and wants a relationship with her. God sent His son Jesus Christ to die on the cross for our sins – so we could have that relationship with Him. If we simply admit we are sinners, believe that Christ died for our sins and confess our sins, we will have eternal life. It's that simple.

I have never had anyone listen to me so intently as I talked. I felt like she was looking into my very heart. If I had been faking what I believe, I know she would have detected that. How grateful I am that I can present my God with confidence and conviction.

Once she and I were talking about the church services the day before. I said that we have a small church (in Mongolian of course). She said "No! You have a small church building. You have a large faith." I told her she was absolutely correct. What a thrill that even in her lost condition and from her Buddhist background, she could see the power of God working in us.

At the time of this writing, although she occasionally attends church, she still has not become a Christian. She remains on my prayer list.

As a Lamb to the Slaughter

One Sunday morning I watched a man put three sheep into the trunk of his car in front of our building. He tied their legs together and plopped them in. They never made a sound! If you had tried to tie the legs of three dogs and put them in the trunk, it would have been a major, noisy production. (If you have ever tried to give a dog a bath, you understand.) But the sheep never made a sound. After they were put in the trunk, they would raise their head and look out but never squirm or wiggle or try to get loose.

Another time we were in the countryside and watched a man kill a sheep for our dinner. The sheep just lay there while the man cut its throat – without uttering a single bleat. Amazing!

I thought about how the Bible describes our Lord as a lamb.

He was oppressed, and he was afflicted, yet he opened not his mouth: he is brought as a lamb to the slaughter, and as a sheep before her shearers is dumb, so he openeth not his mouth.
Isaiah 53:7

In John, Jesus is called the Lamb of God. All my life I've heard preachers and teachers talk about the nature of sheep, but seeing the behavior of sheep in real life somehow made it all more real and more meaningful! I now understand far better all those scriptures about sheep!

So living here is like one continuous lesson. I'm doing better in Reality Scriptures 101 than I am in Mongolian 201.

Oh Father! Let me see the world as you see it! And may I never forget the scenes that have touched my heart.

Chapter Nineteen

THE REST OF THE STORY

Like Paul Harvey, I would love to tell you the rest of this story – but I haven't lived it yet!

We have felt an urgency about this ministry from the very beginning. We did not have time to take a survey trip. We just came. We did not have time to do deputation for 18 months. We just came. We don't know why we feel such an urgency. Maybe this window of opportunity will soon be closed. Maybe we are going to get old and sick. Maybe the Lord is coming back soon. It makes no difference the reason, we know we must work now *for the night cometh, when no man can work. John 9:4b*

Pray for Missionaries

There are so many missionaries and all of them request your prayers. How is a person to know exactly who to pray for? Well, we have the answer! Now you are probably thinking we are going to say "Pray for Mongolian Missions", but that is not the answer. There are two kinds of missionaries who need your prayers.

First, if you read a missionary's report and no one is being saved or added to the work, then you need to pray for that missionary. It is very discouraging to work hard, plant seed, plow the soil around the seed, water the ground, keep weeds away - and yet the ground remains barren. But planting and watering are just as important as harvesting. In fact there will be no harvest without that preliminary work. Pray for the "planting, watering" missionaries that they do not become *weary in well-doing: for in due season (they) shall reap, if (they) faint not. Galatians 6:9*

Second, if you read a missionary's report and God is blessing in a mighty way with souls being saved, you might think you can direct your prayers elsewhere because wonderful blessings are already being poured out. But definitely pray for that missionary at that time. Satan is never happy when God is making changes in people's lives and he will do everything he can to put a stop to such activity. The easiest way is to discourage the missionary. So the greater the blessings, the stronger the resistance from the evil one.

So there you have it! And remember if you "happen" to think about a missionary that just might be God prompting you to pray for that person. What you think is just your nightly visit to the bathroom might be just the time that missionary on the backside of the earth needs prayer. You don't have to remain up the rest of the night knocking down the doors of heaven with your prayers (unless God leads you to do that). A short, simple prayer sincerely uttered touches the heart of God more than hours of flowery, empty words.

God bless you as you pray for missionaries around the world!

Fringe Benefits

Hal and I had careers with great benefit packages, but the fringe benefits of going on the foreign mission field are absolutely awesome! If people only knew, they would immediately join in. No matter how spiritual you might have been in the States (or thought you might have been), your relationship with your Lord becomes closer and more intimate when you commit your life, your energies and your focus to spreading the gospel. And we are living proof that you don't have to be an ordained minister to answer this call. We believe there is a place for missionary helpers on every field.

Oh how honored we are to have been called. Oh how happy we are that we answered that call.

The Rest of the Story

*The harvest truly is plenteous, but the laborers are few.
Pray ye therefore the Lord of the harvest, that he will
send forth laborers into his harvest.
Matthew 9:37-38*

Printed in the United States
1019800003BA/58-1059